First published in Great Britain 1984 by Colour Library Books Ltd.
© Illustrations and text: Colour Library Books Ltd.,
   Guildford, Surrey, England.
Display and text filmsetting by Acesetters Ltd.,
   Richmond, Surrey, England.
Colour separations by Llovet S.A., Barcelona, Spain.
Printed and bound in Barcelona, Spain by Rieusset and Gráficas Estella.
Edited by Anne D. Ager
Stylist: Sarah Whitelock
Coordination: Hanni Edmonds
ISBN 0 86283 257 8

Text by
Lalita Ahmed

Photography by
Peter Barry

Designed by
Philip Clucas

Produced by
Ted Smart and Gerald Hughes

Editorial Direction
David Gibbon

INDIAN COOKING

COLOUR LIBRARY BOOKS

Contents

Introduction
pages 6 and 7

Sherbets and Snacks
pages 8 - 17

Meat, Poultry and Fish
pages 18 - 33

Vegetables, Pulses and Chutney
pages 34 - 47

Bread and Rice
pages 48 - 57

Sweets
pages 58 - 62

Glossary
page 63

Index
page 64

Omelette (far left), Khageea (centre) and Egg Curry (right).

Introduction

India is a vast country with a greatly varied climate and terrain. Each of its many regions boasts its own special style and flavour of cooking, just as each has its own, quite different, language and customs. For example, the same simple vegetable dish may be made in 1,000 different ways by the various castes and regions of India. In Kashmir, which lies in the north, it will be mild and saffron will feature in the preparation. In Uttar Pradesh, which includes the foothills of the Himalayas, it will be simple with a subtle taste. In Delhi-Haryana it will be made in the exotic Mogul style, rich and creamy. In the south of India, in Tamil Nadu, the same dish will become spicy and pungent, for this is the major spice-growing area. Incidentally, the curry which we know today derives from the Keres, a dish characteristic of this southern area. Similarly, the coastal regions of India show a preference for fish and seafood. I have tried to include recipes in this book from all the regions of India.

Indian cooking has developed from a purely vegetarian style to today's mixed style; in the process artistically absorbing the culinary styles of all the subcontinent's past invaders, who have included Persians, Greeks, Romans, Mongols, French, Portuguese and British.

Curry, as we know it today, was introduced to Europe, especially to Britain, by army officers returning from India. They asked their cooks, or *khansamas*, to make a mixture of spices which could be taken home to Europe and used to make the dish for which they had developed a taste while in India. This mixture of spices was named curry powder. Curry quickly became a dish associated with life in India. The demand increased rapidly and some companies set themselves up to export this mixture to Europe. Some ardent curry lovers even went so far as to bring their cooks back from India with them.

After the independence, and partition, of India there was a mass exodus of people to Great Britain, Africa and other parts of the world. They took with them their eating habits and spices, and soon Africa was cultivating those same spices. The mass migration of Asians in the 1960s and 1970s, from East Africa and the Indian subcontinent to Great Britain and other parts of Europe, brought Indian food to the notice of everyone. Suddenly it became as much a part of the British way of life as a cup of tea.

It is no longer strange to find curry included in the menu of the average family. Although it is sometimes thought that curry, with all its spices, is bad for your health, nothing could be further from the truth, for the spices are there to do exactly the opposite. The combination of various spices is there, not only to complement the flavour and enhance the taste, but also to help in the digestion of food. They act as a kind of catalyst, helping the natural enzymes to digest the food. The only spice which is included in a dish purely to add pungency is chilli. Even so, every recipe can be modified according to your own taste by decreasing, increasing or even totally omitting a spice altogether. Similarly, the quantity of cooking oil, ghee or fat can be varied to one's liking.

There is one factor which, above all, makes Indian cooking stand out in the success chart. No matter how inexperienced the cook, or whether the recipe has been correctly followed or not, the ultimate result will always be at least edible. The skill is in making the dish a masterpiece, and that is where individual artistry and imagination play their part. No other style of cooking, except perhaps Chinese, allows such enormous room for flexibility. You can increase or reduce the spices to suit your own palate and it is possible to produce an excellent dish even if one or more spices are not available. Therefore, it is not surprising that, given the same ingredients, four different cooks could produce four different tasting curries. It is the blending of the spices which plays the most important role. This great flexibility has allowed me to take into account the vegetables most readily available in the European and American markets.

Indian food is always colourful, but its beauty is enhanced by the garnishing. Chopped chilli, coriander leaves and artistically cut vegetables - like carrots, cucumbers and radishes - are used freely.

Eating is always an occasion in an Indian household, and so it should be. Sharing a table and food symbolises harmony, love and togetherness, so Indian meals are particularly geared for sharing. If a meal is cooked with four to six people in mind, it could easily stretch to eight or ten people if friends happen to drop by unexpectedly.

Indian meals are not served in different courses, like European meals. All the dishes are served at the same time, with the exception of the sweets. The meals are traditionally served either by the most senior lady in the house or by the mistress of the house. These days, however, it is increasingly the fashion to help yourself.

The dishes featured in this book will take you from Kashmir in the north to the southernmost tip of India. I hope this book will not only help to guide you in the pleasures of Indian cooking, but also to give you a better understanding of spices and their many and varied uses. Happy cooking!

Rasgulla (top left), Paneer Ki Kheer (left) and Jallebi (right).

Sherbets and Snacks

Lassi
(YOGURT SHERBET)

PREPARATION TIME: 5-7 minutes

300ml (½ pint) natural yogurt
50g (2oz) sugar
Pinch of salt
1 litre (1¾ pints) water
Pinch of saffron
10ml (2 tsp) lemon juice
Ice cubes

In a mixing bowl beat yogurt well, add sugar and salt, beat again and add water. Dissolve sugar by stirring well. Add saffron and lemon juice and serve with ice cubes.

Tandi Masala Chaaey
(SPICED ICED TEA)

PREPARATION TIME: 10 minutes.

600ml (1 pint) water
1 teabag or
10ml or 2 tsp orange peko tea leaves
Sugar to taste
4 cloves
2.5cm (1 inch) cinnamon stick
4 small cardamoms, seeds removed and ground
Crushed ice
Fresh lemon juice

Boil 150ml (¼ pint) of water. Put tea, sugar, cloves, cinnamon stick and crushed cardamom seeds in a teapot. Pour in boiling water and allow to stand for 2-4 minutes. Stir well, strain and mix with remaining cold water. Allow to cool. Mix and serve in tall glasses with crushed ice and lemon juice to taste.

This page: Lassi (left), Mint Barley (centre) and Tandi Masala Chaaey (right).

Facing page: Badam Ka Sherbet (left), Lemon Sherbet (centre) and Spiced Grape Sherbet (right).

(Normally served before the meal)

Green Mango Sherbet

PREPARATION TIME: 10-12 minutes

2 green, unripened mangoes
1 litre (1¾ pints) water
Pinch of salt
Sugar to taste
Crushed ice

Boil mangoes for 10 minutes. Remove from water and cool. Remove skin gently. Scrape all the pulp from around the stone and skin. Dissolve pulp in water. Add salt and sugar. Stir well to mix. Serve on a bed of ice.

Mint Barley

PREPARATION TIME: 15 minutes

600-750ml (1-1¼ pints) water
75g or 3oz broken barley
6-8 mint leaves, finely chopped
Pinch of salt
Sugar to taste
Fresh lemon juice

Boil 300ml (½ pint) water and add barley. Simmer for 5 minutes. Strain and discard barley. Add remaining water and finely chopped mint leaves. Add salt and sugar to taste. Chill and serve on ice with lemon juice.

Lemon Sherbet

PREPARATION TIME: 5 minutes

Sugar to taste
Pinch of salt
1.2 litres (2 pints) water
Juice of 2 lemons
5ml (1 tsp) grated lemon rind
Few mint leaves, bruised
Ice cubes

Dissolve sugar and salt in water. Add lemon juice and lemon rind. Add mint leaves and stir well. Serve in tall glasses with ice. 120ml (4 fl oz) of gin or vodka may be added.

Spiced Grape Sherbet

PREPARATION TIME: 10 minutes

225g (8oz) white seedless grapes
100g (4oz) black grapes, seeded
2 cloves
1 litre (1¾ pints) water
Pinch of salt
6 small cardamoms, seeds removed
    and crushed
Sugar to taste
10ml (2 tsp) lemon juice
Pinch of freshly ground pepper
Pinch of ground cinnamon
Crushed ice

Wash grapes and liquidise with cloves, strain through a sieve to collect juice. Add 1 cup/8 fl oz water to grapes and strain once again to collect the juice. Mix grape juice with remaining water and dissolve salt, crushed cardamom seeds and sugar. Add lemon juice, pepper and cinnamon. Mix well. Serve on crushed ice.

Passion Fruit Sherbet

PREPARATION TIME: 10 minutes

8-10 passion fruits
750ml (1¼ pints) water
Sugar
Pinch of salt
1-2 drops of red food colouring
    (optional)
Ice cubes

Cut passion fruits in half. Remove the pulp and blend with the water. Strain and dissolve sugar; add salt. Add red food colouring, if desired, this will make the sherbet pink. Serve with ice cubes.

Blackcurrant Sherbet

PREPARATION TIME: 10 minutes

100-175g or 4-6oz fresh or frozen
    blackcurrants
750ml (1¼ pints) water
50-60g or 2-3oz sugar
Pinch of salt
15ml (1 tblsp) lemon juice
Ice cubes

Mash blackcurrants in a bowl or blend them in a liquidiser. Add water and mix well, then strain. Dissolve sugar and salt and add lemon juice. Serve with ice cubes.

Badam Ka Sherbet
(ALMOND SHERBET)

PREPARATION TIME: 10 minutes

450ml (¾ pint) milk
150ml (¼ pint) water
60g (2½oz) sugar
15g (½oz) blanched almonds, soaked
    in water
15g (½oz) pistachio nuts, soaked
    and skins removed
Pinch of saffron
6 small cardamoms, seeds removed
    and crushed
3-4 drops rosewater
Ice cubes

Mix milk and water and dissolve sugar. Liquidise almonds and pistachio nuts with a little diluted milk. Dissolve saffron, add crushed seeds of cardamom and add rose essence. Serve with ice cubes or well chilled.

Dahi - Wada
(DAAL DUMPLINGS IN YOGURT)

PREPARATION TIME: 5 minutes
and 1 hour for soaking

COOKING TIME: 30 minutes

100g (4oz) urid daal, washed and
    soaked for 1 hour
50g (2oz) moong daal, washed and
    soaked for 1 hour
2.5ml (½ tsp) salt

2.5cm (1 inch) ginger root, peeled
    and finely chopped
1.25ml (¼ tsp) chilli powder or
2 green chillis, finely chopped
50g (2oz) mixed sultanas and raisins
Oil for deep frying

For Yogurt Sauce:
450-600ml (¾-1 pint) natural yogurt
1.25ml (¼ tsp) salt
2.5ml (½ tsp) cumin seed
Water to dip fried wada
2 sprigs coriander, chopped for
    garnish

Blend drained urid daal and moong daal with sufficient water in a liquidiser to make a very thick purée. Put liquidized urid and moong daal into mixing bowl, add salt, ginger, chillis and mixed fruits. Mix well. Heat oil for deep frying. Add small spoonfuls of the mixture to the hot oil to make small dumplings. To make more uniform wadas, you could wet your hands in water and form a little mixture into a flat, round shape before gently lowering the mixture into the oil. Fry both sides for 3-4 minutes or until golden brown. Drain on kitchen paper. Make all the wadas in this way. Mix yogurt and salt together. Soak fried wadas in water for 2-3 minutes. Gently squeeze out any excess water, arrange in a flat serving dish. Pour the yogurt evenly over them. In a hot frying pan, dry roast cumin and coriander seeds for 1-2 minutes. Place the roasted spices in folded

kitchen paper and, with a rolling pin, coarsely grind to a powder. Sprinkle ground spice mixture over the yogurt. Garnish with chopped, fresh green coriander. Alternatively, sprinkle with a pinch of paprika powder.

Pakoras or Bhajias
(DEEP FRIED CHICK PEA FLOUR FRITTERS)

PREPARATION TIME: 15 minutes

COOKING TIME: 10 minutes

100g (4oz) baisen flour (chick pea
    flour)
Pinch of salt
2.5ml (½ tsp) chilli powder
2.5ml (½ tsp) bicarbonate of soda
Water to make batter
Oil for deep frying

Vegetables and Fruits
1 small potato, peeled and sliced into
    ⅛ inch thick wafers
1 small aubergine, cut into thin slices
1 small onion, sliced
1 green pepper, seeded and sliced into
    rings
3-4 florets of cauliflower, separated
    into smaller pieces

Mix baisen flour, salt, chilli powder and soda and make a medium consistency batter with water. Mix well and allow to stand for 3-4 minutes. Heat oil for deep frying. Dip prepared vegetables one by one into the batter, coat well and fry them a few at a time for 4-5 minutes in hot oil until golden brown on both sides. Drain well. Serve hot or cold with chutney.

Other suggestions:
Pineapple rings, apples, tomatoes, spinach leaves, green chillis, bread slices cut in quarter, semi-ripe bananas, sweet potatoes, swede, parsnips, chicken and fish pieces.

This page: Blackcurrant Sherbet (centre) and Passion Fruit Sherbet (right).

Facing page: Pakoras (top), Ghoogni (centre left) and Dahi Wada (bottom).

Crispy Rolls or Curry Patties

PREPARATION TIME: 1 hour

COOKING TIME: 30 minutes

225-275g (8-10oz) plain flour
Salt
15ml (1 tblsp) cornflour
1.25ml (¼ tsp) bicarbonate of soda
25g (1oz) butter or margarine
Water
Paste

Take 2 tsp (10ml) flour and a little water to make a thick paste. Crispy rolls can be made with either a vegetable or meat filling. The rolls themselves are made in the same way for either filling. Sift flour, salt, cornflour and soda. Rub in butter. Make dough with water. Knead well and leave to stand for 10 minutes. Knead once again and divide into 4-6 portions. Roll each portion as thinly as possible on a lightly floured surface. Then cut 10cm (4 inch) squares. Heat frying pan and cook on both sides for ½ minute each. Make the rest similarly. Take a square wrapper and place a little filling slightly above one corner and fold corner over the filling. Bring the two side corners over as if to make the folds of an envelope. Secure with a little water and flour paste and press to seal. Roll over the folded edge to make a neat roll. Seal the flap with water and flour paste. Make all the rolls. Heat oil and fry a few at a time until golden brown. Drain on kitchen paper and serve hot with either chutney or tomato ketchup.

Vegetable Filling
1 onion
30ml (2 tblsp) oil
450g (1lb) potatoes, peeled and cubed
100g (4oz) shelled or frozen peas
Salt
5ml (1 tsp) ground black pepper
Oil for deep frying

Fry onion, in 30ml (2 tblsp) oil for 3-4 minutes. Add cubed boiled potatoes, peas and sprinkle with salt and pepper. Mix well and cook for 3-4 minutes. Cover and allow to cool.

Meat Filling
15ml (1 tblsp) oil
1 onion, peeled and sliced thinly
50g (2oz) grated cabbage
50g (2oz) grated carrots
50g (2oz) sliced green beans
50g (2oz) frozen peas
Salt
2.5ml (½ tsp) ground black pepper
50g (2oz) sprouted beans
225g (8oz) cooked meat (any kind) shredded
10-15ml (2-3 tsp) lemon juice

Heat oil and fry onions for 2 minutes. Add cabbage and carrots and fry for 3 minutes. Add green beans, peas and sprinkle with salt and black pepper. Cover and cook for 4-5 minutes. Add sprouted beans and stir fry for 2 minutes. Add shredded meat. Mix well, add lemon juice and stir the mixture. Cook for 2-3 minutes. Remove from heat, cool and use for filling.

Aloo-Bonda (POTATO BALLS IN BATTER)

PREPARATION TIME: 20 minutes

COOKING TIME: 15 minutes

Batter
100g (4oz) baisen flour (chick pea flour)
Salt
Pinch of baking powder
1.25ml (¼ tsp) chilli powder
150ml (¼ pint) water
Oil for deep frying

Filling
450g (1lb) potatoes, boiled, peeled and cubed
1 onion, peeled and chopped
2 sprigs fresh green coriander, chopped
2.5cm (1 inch) ginger root, peeled and finely chopped
1-2 green chillis, chopped
15ml (1 tbsp) lemon juice or freshly ground black pepper to taste
Salt
10ml (2 tsp) dry mango powder

Sift flour and salt together with baking powder and chilli powder. Add water and mix well to make a smooth batter. If the batter is too thick add a little extra water; if thin add extra sifted baisen flour. Put aside to rest. In a large bowl, put cubed potatoes, chopped onions, coriander, ginger, chillis and lemon juice, mix well and sprinkle with pepper, salt and mango powder. Mix well and take a small lump to form a smooth ball, the size of a golf ball. Mould remaining mixture in the same way. Heat oil and dip potato bonda in baisen batter, coat well and slide them into the oil. Fry a few at a time until the bonda are golden brown. Drain on kitchen paper and serve hot with chutney. Aloo-bondas can be eaten cold, but they do not freeze well.

Dokhala

PREPARATION TIME: Overnight for soaking and 10-12 hours for fermenting.

COOKING TIME: 30-40 minutes

450g (1lb) channa daal (split chick pea), washed
1-2 green chillis
2.5cm (1 inch) ginger root, peeled and sliced
Salt to taste
Pinch of asafoetida
5ml (1 tsp) bicarbonate of soda
60ml (3½ fl oz) oil
6-8 curry leaves
2.5ml (½ tsp) mustard seed
45ml (3 tblsp) fresh grated coconut
2 sprigs coriander leaves, chopped

Soak channa daal overnight. Drain and grind with a little water, the green chillis and ginger to a coarse paste. Beat with a circular motion to incorporate air and leave to ferment for 10-12 hours (use a warm place like an airing cupboard and cover the pan). After it has fermented add salt, asafoetida, soda and half the oil. If too thick, add 30ml (2 tblsp) water. Beat again. Grease a flat 5-6cm (2-2½ inch) deep pie dish with oil. Spread the mixture on it about 2.5cm (1 inch) thick. Steam over a large saucepan for 15-20 minutes. Allow to cool slightly. Heat remaining oil, add curry leaves and mustard seeds and pour over dokhala evenly. Serve garnished with grated coconut and chopped coriander leaves, cut dokhala into 2.5cm (1 inch) square pieces. Dokhala can be frozen for future use.

Khari Sevian (SAVOURY MINCE VERMICELLI)

PREPARATION TIME: 10 minutes

COOKING TIME: 20 minutes for mince and 10 minutes for sevian

1 onion, peeled and finely chopped
25g (1oz) ghee or
22ml (1½ tblsp) oil
2.5ml (½ tsp) ginger paste
1.25ml (¼ tsp) garlic paste
225g (8oz) lamb or beef mince

Salt
5ml (1 tsp) ground black pepper
50g (2oz) butter
225g (8oz) vermicelli, broken into
   smaller pieces
Juice of 1 lemon

Fry onion in ghee or oil for 3-4
minutes. Add ginger, garlic, mince
and salt. Fry for 6-7 minutes. Add
ground black pepper. Mix well.
Cover and cook until mince is dry.
Remove from heat and put aside.
In a non-stick pan, heat butter and
fry vermicelli for 1-2 minutes. Add
cooked mince and stir fry for 1
minute. Add 300ml (½ pint) water.
Cook until dry. Sprinkle with
lemon juice and serve hot.

Khari Sevian (far left), Aloo Bonda (below), Crispy Rolls (centre) and Dokhala (bottom).

Ghoogni
(GREEN PEA FRY OR SPICED GREEN PEAS)

PREPARATION TIME: 5 minutes
COOKING TIME: 10 minutes

1 onion, peeled and chopped
25g (1oz) ghee or
15ml (1 tblsp) oil
2 green chillis, cut in half
2.5cm (1 inch) ginger root, peeled and chopped
450g (1lb) shelled or frozen peas
1.25ml (¼ tsp) black ground pepper
2 sprigs fresh green coriander, chopped
1.25ml (¼ tsp) salt
Juice of 1 lemon

Fry onion in ghee or oil until tender (2-3 minutes), add green chillis and ginger. Fry for 1 minute and add green peas. Stir and cook for 5-6 minutes. Add black pepper, chopped coriander and salt. Cook for a further 2 minutes. Pour into a serving dish and sprinkle with lemon juice. Serve hot with tea.

Samosa
(DEEP FRIED STUFFED SAVOURY PASTRIES)

PREPARATION TIME: 30 minutes
COOKING TIME: 15 minutes

100-150g (4-5oz) plain flour
Pinch of salt
2.5ml (½ tsp) baking powder
25g (1oz) ghee or
22ml (1½ tblsp) oil
Water to mix

Flour paste
15ml (1 tblsp) flour mixed with little water to form thick paste
Oil for deep frying

Samosas may be made with either a vegetable or meat filling. The samosas are made in the same way for either filling. Sift flour and salt and add baking powder. Rub in ghee or oil and add the water, a little at a time, to form a dough. Knead well and set aside. When the filling has been made, knead dough again and make 16-20 even-sized balls. On lightly floured surface roll each ball into a thin circle 10-13cm (4-5 inch) round. Cut across the centre and apply the flour paste along the straight edge and bring the two corners together, overlapping slightly to make a cone. Secure by pressing the pasted edges together. Fill the cone with the filling, apply paste to the open mouth and seal the edge. Prepare the rest of the samosas in the same way. Heat oil. When it is moderately hot, fry samosas, a few at a time, until golden brown. Drain on kitchen paper and serve hot or cold with a sweet chutney or plain tomato ketchup.

For Vegetable Filling
15ml (1 tblsp) oil
1 onion, peeled and chopped
10ml (2 tsp) garam masala powder
2.5ml (½ tsp) salt
2.5ml (½ tsp) chilli powder
450g (1lb) potatoes, boiled, peeled, cubed and boiled for 4 to 5 minutes
50g (2oz) frozen or shelled peas
10ml (2 tsp) dry mango powder
Lemon juice

To make filling, heat oil and fry onion until just tender. Sprinkle with garam masala, salt and chilli powder. Fry for one minute and add drained potatoes and peas. Mix well and fry for 2-3 minutes until potatoes are tender. Sprinkle with mango powder or lemon juice. Allow to cool.

Meat Filling
1 onion, peeled and chopped
50g (2oz) ghee or
30ml (2 tblsp) oil
450g (1lb) mince (lamb or beef)
5ml (1 tsp) ginger paste
5ml (1 tsp) garlic paste
10ml (2 tsp) ground black pepper
2.5ml (½ tsp) salt

Fry onion until golden brown in ghee or oil. Add mince, ginger and garlic paste, black ground pepper and salt. Fry the mixture for 8-10 minutes until dry. Remove from pan and allow to cool. Samosas made with mince can be frozen either half fried or unfried. Fry straight from the freezer when required. They can also be thawed before frying without any damage or alteration to taste.

Tikia
(POTATO-MINCE PATTIES)

PREPARATION TIME: 20 minutes
COOKING TIME: 20-30 minutes

1 onion, peeled and chopped
25g (1oz) ghee or
15ml (1 tblsp) oil
225g (8oz) minced lamb or beef
100g (4oz) frozen or shelled peas
2 sprigs fresh green coriander leaves, chopped
2-3 small green chillis, chopped (optional)
5ml (1 tsp) ground black pepper
450g (1lb) boiled potatoes, peeled and mashed
5-10ml (1-2 tsp) salt
1-2 beaten eggs
Oil for frying

Fry onion in ghee or oil until just tender (2-3 minutes). Add mince, peas, coriander leaves, chillis and black pepper. Fry for 4-5 minutes. Cool and mix with mashed potatoes and salt. Make 20-25 small, flat burger shapes. Heat the oil in a frying pan and dip tikias in beaten egg to coat. Shallow fry in hot oil. Fry on each side for 2-3 minutes. Serve hot or cold with chutney.

Khageea
(SPICED SCRAMBLED EGG)

PREPARATION TIME: 6 minutes
COOKING TIME: 10 minutes

1 onion, peeled and chopped
30ml (2 tblsp) oil
2.5ml (½ tsp) chilli powder
1.25ml (¼ tsp) turmeric powder
1 green chilli, chopped
2 sprigs fresh coriander leaves, chopped
2 fresh tomatoes, chopped
Salt to taste
15ml (1 tblsp) water
4 well-beaten eggs

Fry onion in oil for 2 minutes. Add spices and green chilli and coriander leaves, stir fry for 1 minute. Add chopped, fresh tomatoes. Season with salt and sprinkle in the water. Add beaten eggs. Cover and cook on gentle heat for 6-7 minutes. Stir and mix egg over gentle heat. Khageea should look like spiced scrambled eggs. Serve with parathas for any meal, including a hearty breakfast.

Wada
(DAAL FRITTERS)

PREPARATION TIME: 2-3 hours
COOKING TIME: 20 minutes

100g (4oz) urid daal, washed and soaked for 2-3 hours
100g (4oz) yellow, dehusked moong daal, washed and soaked for 2-3 hours
Little water to grind
1 onion, peeled and finely chopped
5-10ml (1-2 tsp) salt
2-3 sprigs fresh coriander leaves, chopped
1 small green chilli finely chopped or
2.5ml (½ tsp) chilli powder
2.5cm (1 inch) ginger root, peeled and finely chopped
1.25ml (¼ tsp) bicarbonate of soda
Oil for deep frying

Grind drained urid and moong daal with a little water to a coarse, thick paste. Pour into a mixing bowl and add onion, salt, coriander leaves, chilli powder or green chillis, ginger and soda. Mix well and set aside for 4-5 minutes. Fry small spoonfuls of the mixture, a few at a time, for 3-4 minutes until golden brown. Drain and serve hot with chutney.

Omelette

PREPARATION TIME: 5 minutes
COOKING TIME: 5 minutes

2 eggs per person, white and yolk separated
1 small onion, finely chopped
1 fresh tomato, thinly sliced
1 green chilli, finely chopped
1 sprig coriander leaves, finely chopped
5ml (1 tsp) water
Salt to taste
15ml (1 tblsp) oil

Beat egg white until stiff. Add egg yolk and beat well. Mix in chopped onion, tomato, chilli, coriander and water. Grease a frying pan well with oil. Heat the pan and pour the egg mixture into it. Sprinkle with salt to taste. Cover and cook the omelette for 2-3 minutes until the sides leave the pan. With a flat

Facing page: Tikia (top left), Samosa (top right) and Wada (bottom).

spoon or spatula ease the base of the omelette and turn it over to cook the other side. Cover and cook for another 2-3 minutes. Serve hot with tomato ketchup or chutney, along with rotis or parathas.

Ganthia
(BAISEN STICKS)

PREPARATION TIME: 10 minutes

COOKING TIME: 10-15 minutes

225g (8oz) baisen flour (chick pea flour)
1.25-2.5ml (¼-½ tsp) salt
2.5ml (½ tsp) bicarbonate of soda
2.5ml (½ tsp) omum (ajwain)
20 whole peppercorns, crushed
Pinch of asafoetida
50ml (2½ fl oz) oil
Oil for frying
Water

Sift flour, salt, bicarbonate of soda and omum together. Add crushed peppercorns, asafoetida and 30ml (1½ fl oz) warm oil. Rub in well and knead with water to make a stiff dough. Take 5ml (1 tsp) oil, rub over dough and knead. Repeat 3-4 times until dough is quiet smooth. Pass lumps of dough, through sev mould or spaghetti machine, with a large hole setting. Fry baisen sticks in hot oil until golden brown and crisp over a low heat. Drain on kitchen paper and store in airtight containers. Serve with tea or drinks.

Egg Curry

PREPARATION TIME: 10 minutes

COOKING TIME: 20 minutes

1 large onion, peeled and chopped
25g (1oz) ghee or
15ml (1 tblsp) oil
2.5cm (1 inch) cinnamon stick
1 bayleaf
4 small cardamoms
6 cloves
5ml (1 tsp) garlic paste
5ml (1 tsp) ginger paste
5ml (1 tsp) ground coriander
5ml (1 tsp) ground cumin
1.25ml (¼ tsp) turmeric powder
5ml (1 tsp) garam masala powder
5ml (1 tsp) chilli powder
200-225g (7-8oz) canned tomatoes, crushed
Salt to taste
175ml (6 fl oz) water
4-6 eggs, hard boiled and shelled
2 sprigs fresh green coriander leaves, chopped
2 green chillis, chopped

Fry onion in oil for 2-3 minutes. Add cinnamon, bayleaf, cardamoms, cloves. Fry for 1 minute. Add ginger and garlic paste. Stir the mixture, add coriander, cumin, turmeric, garam masala and chilli powder. Add canned tomatoes and salt to taste. Cook the spices for 5 minutes. Add water, cover and bring to boil. Add eggs and cook for 10-12 minutes. Garnish with green chillis and fresh coriander leaves. The gravy can be increased or reduced as required. Serve with plain boiled rice.

Nimki and Papadi

PREPARATION TIME: 10 minutes

COOKING TIME: 15-20 minutes

225g (8oz) plain flour
1.25g (¼ tsp) salt
2.5ml (½ tsp) bicarbonate of soda
5ml (1 tsp) onion seed (kalongi)
2.5ml (½ tsp) omum
Pinch of asafoetida
50g (2oz) ghee or
45ml (3 tblsp) oil
Water
Oil for deep frying

Sift flour, salt, bicarbonate of soda, and add onion seed and omum. Add asafoetida and rub in ghee or oil. Knead with water to make a stiff dough. Knead for 3-4 minutes until smooth. Make 2 equal portions. Roll out each portion as thinly as possible, to about 3mm (⅛ inch) thickness. Then cut the first piece of dough diagonally into strips both ways to make small bite size diamond shapes and prick with fork. Roll out the other dough to a similar thickness and cut neat, round shapes with a clean, sharp jar lid or a biscuit cutter. Heat the oil and fry the shapes until golden brown and crisp. Drain on kitchen paper and allow to cool before storing them in jars or tins. These can be stored for up to 2 months. Serve with tea or drinks. The diamond shapes are called nimki and the round shapes are called papadi.

Ganthia (top) and Nimki and Papadi (bottom).

Meat, Poultry and Fish

Bhoona Gosht

PREPARATION TIME: 15 minutes
COOKING TIME: 1 hour

1 onion, peeled and chopped
45ml (3 tblsp) oil or
40g (1½oz) ghee
2.5cm (1 inch) cinnamon stick
6 small cardamoms
1 bayleaf
6 cloves
3 large cardamoms
5ml (1 tsp) ginger paste
5ml (1 tsp) garlic paste
450g (1lb) braising steak or lamb or
    beef, cubed
10ml (2 tsp) ground coriander
10ml (2 tsp) ground cumin
5ml (1 tsp) chilli powder
1.25ml (¼ tsp) turmeric powder
4 fresh tomatoes or
1 small can of tomatoes
250ml (8 fl oz) water
Salt to taste
2 green chillis, chopped
2 sprigs fresh coriander, chopped

Fry onions in oil or ghee until light
brown. Add cinnamon,
cardamoms, cloves, bayleaf. Fry for
one minute. Add ginger and garlic
pastes and fry for further one
minute. Add meat and sprinkle
with coriander, cumin, chilli and
turmeric powder. Mix well and fry
for 10 minutes. Add chopped fresh
or canned tomatoes. Season with
salt and add water. Cover and cook
for 40-45 minutes on low heat,
until meat is tender. Add chopped
chillis and coriander.

Kofta Curry

PREPARATION TIME: 15 minutes
COOKING TIME: 30 minutes

450g (1lb) lean minced meat
2.5ml (½ tsp) ginger paste
5ml (1 tsp) garlic paste
1 egg
5ml (1 tsp) ground garam masala
2.5ml (½ tsp) chilli powder

For sauce
1 onion, peeled and finely chopped
30-40g (about 1½oz) ghee or
2-3 tblsp oil

6 small cardamoms
2.5cm (1 inch) stick cinnamon
6 cloves
1 bayleaf
5ml (1 tsp) garlic paste
5ml (1 tsp) ginger paste
5ml (1 tsp) ground cumin
2.5ml (½ tsp) chilli powder
1.25ml (¼ tsp) turmeric powder
10ml (2 tsp) ground coriander
Salt to taste
150ml (¼ pint) plain, natural yogurt
    or
30ml (2 tblsp) tomato purée
600ml (1 pint) water

For garnish
2 green chillis, chopped
2 sprigs fresh coriander, finely
    chopped

Mix mince with ginger, garlic paste
and egg. Add garam masala and
chilli powder. Mix well and make
16-20 even-sized balls. Keep in a
cool place.

Sauce
Fry onion in ghee for 4 minutes
until light golden brown. Add
cardamom, cinnamon, cloves and
bayleaf. Stir fry for one minute.
Add garlic and ginger pastes and fry
for another minute. Sprinkle with
cumin, chilli, turmeric and
coriander. Stir well and add yogurt
or tomato purée. If yogurt is used,
fry the spices until yogurt is dry
and oil separates (5-7 minutes).
Add water, cover and bring to boil.
Add salt. Slide mince balls one at a
time into the saucepan. Shake the
saucepan to settle the mince balls;
do not stir or else the balls will
break. Cover and gently simmer for
20 minutes. Garnish with chopped
chillis and coriander leaves. Serve
with rice or chapatis.

Keema Methi

PREPARATION TIME: 30 minutes
COOKING TIME: 30 minutes

1 onion, peeled and chopped
25g (1oz) ghee or
2 tblsp oil
4 small green cardamoms
2.5cm (1 inch) cinnamon stick
1 bayleaf

6 cloves
5ml (1 tsp) ginger paste
5ml (1 tsp) garlic paste
450g (1lb) lamb or beef mince
5ml (1 tsp) powder chilli
10ml (2 tsp) ground coriander
10ml (2 tsp) ground cumin
1.25ml (¼ tsp) turmeric powder
150ml (¼ pint) natural yogurt
Salt to taste
1 bunch fresh methi leaves, stemmed
    and chopped or
15ml (1 tblsp) dry kasuri methi
    leaves

Fry onion in oil till just tender. Add
cardamoms, cinnamon stick,
bayleaf, cloves and fry for one
minute. Add ginger and garlic
pastes and cook for one minute.
Add mince. Stir the mixture and
sprinkle with chilli, coriander,
cumin and turmeric. Mix well and
cook for 5 minutes. Add well-
stirred yogurt and fresh methi
leaves or dry methi. Cover and
cook till liquid is absorbed. Season
with salt. Serve with chapati or
rice.

Dam Ke Kebab
(BAKED KEBAB)

PREPARATION TIME: 30 minutes
COOKING TIME: 1 hour

450g (1lb) lean mince
5ml (1 tsp) ginger paste
5ml (1 tsp) garlic paste
2 green chillis, ground or finely
    chopped
10ml (2 tsp) garam masala
150ml (¼ pint) natural yogurt
1.25ml (¼ tsp) meat tenderiser
2 sprigs green coriander, finely
    chopped
5ml (1 tsp) chilli powder
2 eggs
1 onion, peeled, thinly sliced and
    fried until crisp
Salt to taste
2 green chillis, chopped
Juice of 1 lemon
Oil

Mix together the mince, ginger,
garlic paste, ground chilli, garam
masala, yogurt, meat tenderiser,
half finely chopped coriander, chilli
powder, eggs and crisply fried

onions. Mix well and season with
salt. In a well-greased baking tray,
spread mince to 1cm (½ inch)
thick. Brush with oil and bake in a
preheated oven Gas Mark 4
(180°C or 350°F) for 20 minutes.
Reduce temperature to Gas Mark
2 (150°C or 300°F) for a further
20-30 minutes or until liquid has
evaporated. Cut into 5cm (2 inch)
squares. Garnish with chopped
chillis and remaining fresh
coriander leaves. Sprinkle with
lemon juice before serving.

Boti-Kebab

PREPARATION TIME: 6 minutes
and 3-4 hours to marinate
COOKING TIME: 30 minutes

450g (1lb) shoulder or leg of lamb,
    cut into bite size pieces
5ml (1 tsp) ginger paste
5ml (1 tsp) garlic paste
5ml (1 tsp) chilli powder
1.25ml (¼ tsp) salt
30ml (2 tblsp) malt vinegar
Juice of ½ a lemon
Oil for basting
1 green pepper
1 large onion, cut into 2.5cm (1 inch)
    pieces
3-4 tomatoes, quartered
6-8 skewers

Mix meat with ginger, garlic, chilli
powder, salt and vinegar and leave
to marinate for 3-4 hours. Sprinkle
with lemon juice and rub spices
well into meat; keep aside. Heat
grill. Thread pieces of meat onto
skewers, alternating them with
tomato, green pepper and onion.
Brush with oil and cook under grill
for 3-4 minutes turning frequently
to cook all sides. Sprinkle with
lemon juice and serve with mixed
salad.

**Facing page: Bhoona Gosht (top
left), Kofta Curry (centre right)
and Keema Methi (bottom).**

Dum Ke Kebab (left), Sheikh Kebab and Boti Kebab, skewered, (centre) and Shami Kebab (right).

Rogan Josh (below).

Rogan Josh
(RICH LAMB WITH NUTS)

PREPARATION TIME: 20 minutes

COOKING TIME: 1 hour

1 onion, peeled and sliced
50g (2oz) ghee or
60ml (4 tblsp) oil
6 green cardamoms
4 large cardamoms
6 cloves
2 bayleaves
2.5cm (1 inch) cinnamon stick
2.5cm (1 inch) root ginger, crushed
3 cloves garlic, crushed
450g (1lb) boned lamb or beef, cut into cubes
5ml (1 tsp) ground cumin
5ml (1 tsp) chilli powder
10ml (2 tsp) paprika powder
5ml (1 tsp) ground coriander
150ml (¼ pint) natural yogurt
5ml (1 tsp) salt
25g (1oz) chopped, blanched almonds
15ml (1 tblsp) posté (poppyseeds), ground
350ml (12 fl oz) water
1 pinch saffron

Fry onion in ghee or oil until lightly browned. Stir fry cardamoms, cloves, bayleaf and cinnamon for 1 minute. Add ginger and garlic paste, stir and add meat. Sprinkle on, one at a time, the cumin, chilli, paprika and coriander powder. Fry the mixture for 2 minutes. Add yogurt and salt; cover and cook for 5-7 minutes until dry and oil separates. Add almonds and poppyseeds. Stir fry for 1-2 minutes and add water. Cover and cook for 40-50 minutes gently simmering until meat is tender and the mixture is fairly dry. Sprinkle with saffron. Cover and gently cook for another 5-10 minutes, taking care not to burn the meat. Stir the mixture a few times to mix saffron. Rogan josh is a dry dish with moist spices around the meat. Serve with pulao, nan or parathas.

Shami Kebab

PREPARATION TIME: 1 hour

COOKING TIME: 10 minutes

450g (1lb) leg of lamb or beef, cubed
300ml (½ pint) water
1 small onion, peeled and thickly sliced
2.5cm (1 inch) ginger root, peeled and sliced
3 cloves of garlic, peeled and chopped
15ml (1 tblsp) channa daal, washed and presoaked in water for 10 minutes
2.5cm (1 inch) cinnamon stick
1 bayleaf, finely crushed
1-2 eggs
Salt
6 cloves, ground
6 small cardamoms, ground
10 whole peppercorns, ground
5ml (1 tsp) whole black cumin, ground
Oil for frying

For filling
1 small onion, peeled and finely sliced
10ml (2 tsp) natural yogurt
Pinch of salt
1 sprig green coriander leaves, chopped

Pressure-cook meat with water, onion, ginger, garlic, channa daal, cinnamon and bayleaf for 15-20 minutes. Remove lid and evaporate remaining liquid. Remove cinnamon stick. Use an electric blender to mix the mixture to a sausage meat consistency. Add egg, season with salt and sprinkle with ground spices. Mix well. Make 10-12 even portions. Mix onions, yogurt and coriander. Take a portion of meat, make a depression in the centre, put a little of the onion yogurt filling in the centre and pat the meat paste into a round, flat shape to enclose the filling (about 5cm (2 inches) in diameter). Continue to make the rest of the shamis similarly. Heat oil in a frying pan and fry them light brown for 2-3 minutes on each side. Serve with lemon wedges, onion salad and pita bread.

Sheikh Kebab

PREPARATION TIME: 30 minutes

COOKING TIME: 20 minutes

450g (1lb) lean minced beef or lamb
1 onion, finely minced
1 green chilli, ground to paste
10ml (2 tsp) kasuri methi
2.5ml (½ tsp) chilli powder
10ml (2 tsp) garam masala powder
1.25ml (¼ tsp) salt
2 sprigs fresh coriander leaves, chopped
5ml (1 tsp) ginger paste
5ml (1 tsp) garlic paste
2 eggs
Oil
Lemon quarters

Picture below: Dum Ka Ran (top) and Masala Chops (bottom).

mixture is dry and oil separates, remove from heat and sprinkle with lemon juice. If the meats become too dry during cooking, add a little water or stock.

Masala Chops

PREPARATION TIME: 15 minutes

COOKING TIME: 20-30 minutes

450g (1lb) lamb chops
150ml (¼ pint) natural yogurt
5ml (1 tsp) garlic paste
5ml (1 tsp) ginger paste
5ml (1 tsp) chilli powder
5ml (1 tsp) ground black pepper
5ml (1 tsp) ground cumin
5ml (1 tsp) salt
Oil for basting
Lemon wedges

Place chops in a bowl and add yogurt, spices and salt. Mix spices well into the chops. Keep aside for 5-6 minutes. Pour on 30ml (2 tblsp) oil and mix well. Spread aluminium baking foil over grill tray. Arrange a few chops and cook them under the grill for 5-6 minutes each side. Baste with oil if required. Alternatively, arrange chops on a baking tray and cook them in preheated oven, Gas Mark 4 (180°C or 350°F) for 30-35 minutes, turning them once. Serve hot with mixed salad and garnished with lemon wedges.

Dum Ka Ran

PREPARATION TIME: 24 hours to marinate

COOKING TIME: 2 hours

2.25-2.75kg (5-6lb) whole leg of lamb
450ml (¾ pint) natural yogurt
45ml (3 tblsp) malt vinegar
5ml (1 tsp) salt
Juice of 2 lemons
10ml (2 tsp) chilli powder
1.25ml (¼ tsp) red food colouring
10ml (2 tsp) garlic paste
10ml (2 tsp) ginger paste
1.25ml (¼ tsp) sugar
Oil for basting
Aluminium foil

Put meat in a large container and make 3-4 1cm (half inch) deep cuts. Mix yogurt, vinegar, salt, lemon juice, chilli powder, food colouring, garlic paste, ginger paste and sugar. Mix well and pour over the meat.

In a bowl mix mince, onion, green chilli, methi, chilli powder, garam masala, salt, coriander, ginger and garlic, mix well. Break in eggs and mix well. Let mixture stand for 10 minutes. Rub a skewer with a little oil. Take some of the mixture and spread it round the skewer to approximately 10cm (4 inch) length. Make the remaining sheikh kebabs and cook them under the grill, brushed with oil, for 3-4 minutes, turning frequently to cook all sides evenly. Serve piping hot with lemon quarters, tamarind pulp or yogurt and mint chutney. A side salad of onions and plain roti goes well with sheikh kebab.

Tali Kaleji/Gurda/Dil (MIXED FRY)

PREPARATION TIME: 15 minutes

COOKING TIME: 40-45 minutes

225g (½ lb) pig's liver, cut into half-inch cubes
4 lambs' kidneys, halved and cored
2 hearts, cored and cut into 2.5cm (1 inch) pieces
5ml (1 tsp) chilli powder
10ml (2 tsp) ground coriander
1.25ml (¼ tsp) turmeric powder
2-3 cloves of garlic or
5ml (1 tsp) garlic paste or
2.5ml (½ tsp) garlic powder
1 root of ginger or

7.5ml (1½ tsp) ginger paste or
6ml (1¼ tsp) ground ginger
40g (1½oz) ghee or
3 tblsp oil
Salt to taste
1 lemon

Rinse all the meats in lightly salted water and remove visible fats and sinew. Drain well and toss in chilli powder, coriander, turmeric powder, ginger and garlic and set aside for 5 minutes. In a 4-5 pint saucepan melt ghee and add the meat mixture. Cook gently for 40-45 minutes, stirring occasionally. Add salt to taste. The colour will change to dark brown. When the

Press well into the cuts and cover the container and refrigerate overnight to marinate. Turn once. Next day remove meat and discard marinade. Wrap in baking foil and cook in a preheated oven Gas Mark 5 (190°C or 375°F) for 1-1¼ hours. Baste occasionally with oil and turn the meat to brown evenly. Reduce heat to Gas Mark 3 (160°C or 325°F) and cook for another 45 minutes. Serve with daal and pulao.

Karai Gosht

PREPARATION TIME: 15 minutes

COOKING TIME: 40-60 minutes

450g (1lb) lean beef, pork or lamb,
  cut into 2.5cm (1 inch) pieces
5ml (1 tsp) chilli powder
5ml (1 tsp) ground cumin
5ml (1 tsp) ground coriander

15ml (1 tblsp) aniseed powder
10ml (2 tsp) kasuri dry methi leaves
150ml (¼ pint) natural yogurt
65g (2½oz) ghee or
4 tblsp oil
1 large onion, peeled and sliced
2 bayleaves
5cm (2 inch) cinnamon sticks
6 cloves
6 small cardamoms
5cm (2 inch) ginger root, peeled and
  crushed
4 cloves of garlic, peeled and crushed
175ml (6 fl oz) water
Salt to taste

In a bowl mix meat with chilli, cumin, coriander, aniseed powder, methi leaves and unsweetened yogurt. Keep aside. Fry onion in oil until tender (4-5 minutes). Add bayleaves, cinnamon, cloves, small cardamoms, ginger and garlic and fry for 2 minutes. Add marinated meat, water and salt to taste. Cover the pan and cook for 30 minutes.

In a wok or non-stick pan transfer the meat and stir fry until the liquid is dry. Add extra water, if needed, a little at a time and keep stir frying until meat is tender. The oil should separate. This is a dry dish.

Meat Do Piaza

PREPARATION TIME: 15 minutes

COOKING TIME: 50-60 minutes

1 small onion, peeled and chopped
50g (2oz) ghee or
45ml (3 tblsp) oil
450g (1lb) shoulder or leg of lamb,
  cubed
5ml (1 tsp) ginger paste
5ml (1 tsp) garlic paste
2.5cm (1 inch) cinnamon stick
6 cloves
6 small cardamoms
5ml (1 tsp) chilli powder

5ml (1 tsp) ground coriander
10ml (2 tsp) ground cumin
150ml (¼ pint) water
Salt to taste
2 large onions, peeled and cut into
  thin rings
Juice of 1 lemon
2 sprigs green fresh coriander leaves,
  chopped
1-2 green chillis
Extra oil if needed

Fry chopped onion in oil or ghee until just tender. Add meat, ginger, garlic, cinnamon, cloves, cardamoms, chilli powder,

This page: Tali Kalegi/Gurda/ Dil (left), Meat Palak (centre right) and Meat Madras (bottom right). Facing page: Meat Do Piaza (top), Korma (centre right) and Karai Gosht (bottom).

coriander and cumin. Fry for 5-6 minutes. Add water and salt to taste. Cook covered for 30-40 minutes on low heat until meat is cooked and liquid has evaporated. Add onion rings. They can be fried in a little extra oil if desired. Stir the meat, cover and cook for a further 10-15 minutes. The onions should be tender. Sprinkle with lemon juice and add green chillis and coriander. This is a dry dish. Serve with pulas or puri.

Meat Palak
(SPINACH MEAT)

PREPARATION TIME: 30-45 minutes

COOKING TIME: 1 hour

50-75g (2-3oz) ghee or
60ml (4 tblsp) oil
1 medium onion, peeled and chopped
1 bayleaf
2.5cm (1 inch) cinnamon stick
4 small cardamoms
6 cloves
2.5cm (1 inch) of root ginger, crushed
3-4 cloves of garlic, crushed
450g lamb or beef, cubed
150ml (¼ pint) natural yogurt
5ml (1 tsp) chilli powder
2.5ml (½ tsp) turmeric powder
10ml (2 tsp) ground coriander
2 green chillis, chopped (optional)
2 sprigs of fresh green coriander, chopped (optional)
450g (1lb) leaf spinach, boiled and puréed (or canned or frozen spinach purée)
Salt to taste

Heat oil and fry onions until light golden brown. Add bayleaf, cinnamon, cardamoms and cloves. Fry for one minute. Add ginger and garlic paste and fry for a further minute. Add meat and yogurt and sprinkle with chilli, turmeric and coriander. Season with salt and cook with the lid on until moisture evaporates (30-40 minutes). Add puréed or canned spinach, mix well and cook for a further 15-20 minutes on a low heat until oil rises to the top. Garnish with chopped chilli and coriander.

Chicken Masala

PREPARATION TIME: 10 minutes and marinate overnight

COOKING TIME: 40-50 minutes plus 10 minutes

1½kg (3lb) chicken, cut into 8-10 pieces
30ml (2 tblsp) oil
150ml (¼ pint) natural yogurt
5ml (1 tsp) ginger
5ml (1 tsp) garlic
10ml (2 tsp) ground cumin
10ml (2 tsp) garam masala powder
5ml (1 tsp) salt
Juice of 1 lemon
10ml (2 tsp) ground black pepper
10ml (2 tsp) ground mango
5ml (1 tsp) kasuri methi
5ml (1 tsp) dry mint powder

Marinate chicken pieces overnight in a well-mixed marinade made from the oil, yogurt, ginger, garlic, cumin, garam masala, salt and lemon juice. Roast chicken with marinade wrapped in baking foil in preheated oven Gas Mark 5 (190°C or 375°F) for 40-50 minutes. Save the liquid and mix with the black pepper, mango powder, methi and mint. Mix well and keep aside. Cool chicken slightly and cut into bite size pieces. Pour in the liquid mixture and mix well. Transfer onto baking tray and bake for further 10-15 minutes until the chicken pieces are dry. Serve as snack or with cocktails.

Meat Madras

PREPARATION TIME: 10 minutes

COOKING TIME: 1 hour

1 onion, peeled and chopped
40g (1½oz) ghee or
45ml (3 tblsp) oil
2cm (¾ inch) cinnamon stick
4 small cardamoms
2 bayleaves
6 fresh curry leaves
6 cloves
15ml (1 tblsp) fresh or desiccated coconut
1.25ml (¼ tsp) fenugreek seeds, crushed
3 cloves garlic, peeled and chopped
2.5cm (1 inch) ginger root, peeled and sliced
450g (1lb) braising steak or lamb, cut into cubes
Salt to taste
5ml (1 tsp) chilli powder
10ml (2 tsp) ground coriander
10ml (2 tsp) ground cumin
1.25ml (¼ tsp) turmeric powder
4 tomatoes, quartered
250ml (8 fl oz) water
2 green chillis, quartered (optional)
2 sprigs fresh green coriander, chopped
Juice of 1 lemon

Fry onion in ghee or oil until just tender (2-3 minutes). Add cinnamon, cardamoms, bayleaves, curry leaves, cloves, coconut, fenugreek seeds, garlic and ginger and fry for 1-2 minutes. Add meat and fry for 3 minutes. Sprinkle with chilli, coriander, cumin, and turmeric. Stir well and add water. Cover and cook for 20 minutes. Add salt, and cook for a further 15-20 minutes until liquid has evaporated. Add tomatoes, chilli and coriander leaves. Cover and cook for 10 minutes on a low heat. Sprinkle with lemon juice. Serve with parathas.

Chicken Tomato

PREPARATION TIME: 30 minutes

COOKING TIME: 40-50 minutes

1 onion, peeled and chopped
45ml (3 tblsp) oil or
40g (1½oz) ghee
2.5cm (1 inch) cinnamon stick
1 bayleaf
6 cloves
6 green cardamoms
2.5cm (1 inch) ginger root, peeled and sliced
4 cloves garlic, peeled and chopped
1½kg (3lb) roasting chicken cut into 8-10 pieces
5ml (1 tsp) chilli powder
5ml (1 tsp) ground cumin
5ml (1 tsp) ground coriander
400g (14oz) canned tomatoes, crushed
5ml (1 tsp) salt
2 sprigs fresh coriander leaves, chopped
2 green chillis, halved

Fry onion for 2 minutes in oil or ghee. Add the cinnamon, bayleaf, cloves, cardamoms for 1 minute then add ginger and garlic. Fry for half a minute. Add chicken pieces. Sprinkle with chilli powder, cumin, coriander. Fry for 2-3 minutes, add crushed tomatoes. Season with salt and add chopped green coriander and chillis. Stir chicken to mix well. Cover and cook for 40-45 minutes until chicken is tender.

Chicken Tandoori
Although the true taste of tandoori (clay oven) is not achieved, a very good result is obtained by baking in an oven.

PREPARATION TIME: 10 minutes and marinate overnight

COOKING TIME: 30-40 minutes

1½kg (3lb) chicken, cut into 8-10 clean pieces
5ml (1 tsp) garlic paste
5ml (1 tsp) ginger paste
5ml (1 tsp) ground black pepper
5ml (1 tsp) paprika
1.25ml (¼ tsp) red food colouring
5ml (1 tsp) salt
45ml (3 tblsp) malt vinegar
Juice of 1 lemon
150ml (¼ pint) natural yogurt
5ml (1 tsp) dry mint powder
Oil
1 lemon, cut into wedges

Mix all the ingredients, apart from the lemon wedges and oil, and marinate chicken pieces in it overnight. Arrange chicken pieces on baking tray. Brush with oil and bake in preheated oven Gas Mark 5 (190°C or 375°F) for 40 minutes, turning them over to achieve even baking. Bake until dry and well browned. Serve with lemon wedges.

Korma

PREPARATION TIME: 15 minutes

COOKING TIME: 40-50 minutes

40g (1½oz) ghee or
45ml (3 tblsp) oil
1 medium onion, peeled and thinly sliced
2.5cm (1 inch) cinnamon stick
6 cloves
6 small cardamoms
1 bayleaf
5ml (1 tsp) small black whole cumin seeds
10ml (2 tsp) ginger paste
5ml (1 tsp) garlic paste
450g (1lb) shoulder of lamb, cubed
5ml (1 tsp) chilli powder
5ml (1 tsp) ground coriander
10ml (2tsp) ground cumin
1.25 ml (¼ tsp) turmeric powder
150ml (¼ pint) natural yogurt
175ml (6 fl oz) water
Salt to taste
2 sprigs fresh coriander, chopped
2 green chillis, halved
15ml (1 tblsp) ground almonds

Facing page: Chicken Tandoori (top), Chicken Tomato (centre right) and Chicken Masala (bottom).

Fry onion in oil or ghee until golden brown. Add cinnamon, cloves, cardamoms, bayleaf and black cumin. Fry for 1 minute, add ginger and garlic paste. Stir for half a minute. Add meat and sprinkle with chilli, coriander, cumin and turmeric powders. Mix well and add yogurt. Cover and cook for 10-15 minutes, occasionally stirring the mixture. Add water, salt to taste and cover. Cook on low temperature for 30-40 minutes or until meat is tender. Korma should have medium-thick gravy. Add ground almonds, green chillis and coriander leaves. Add extra water if needed. Serve with rice or chapatis.

Pork Vindaloo

PREPARATION TIME: 15 minutes

COOKING TIME: 1-1¼ hours

1 large onion, peeled and chopped
50g (2oz) ghee or
45ml (3 tblsp) oil
2.5cm (1 inch) cinnamon stick
6 cloves
6 green cardamoms
5ml (1 tsp) ginger paste
5ml (1 tsp) garlic paste
450g (1lb) lean pork, cut into cubes
45ml (3 tblsp) malt vinegar

5ml (1 tsp) chilli powder
5ml (1 tsp) ground cumin
10ml (2 tsp) ground coriander
30ml (2 tblsp) tamarind pulp
10ml (2 tsp) tomato purée
10ml (2 tsp) sugar
Water
2 sprigs fresh green coriander leaves, chopped
1-2 green chillis, chopped
Salt to taste
15ml (1 tblsp) oil for tempering
6-8 curry leaves

Fry onion in ghee or oil until light brown. Add cinnamon stick, cloves and cardamoms. Fry for half a minute. Add ginger, garlic pastes and pork and fry for 5 minutes or until liquid from pork is dry. Add vinegar and chilli, cumin, coriander, tamarind pulp, tomato purée and sugar. Cover and cook for 10-15 minutes. Add a little water if mixture is dry. Sprinkle with coriander leaves and chopped chilli. Cook on low heat for 30-40 minutes or until pork is tender. The dish should have a rich gravy. Heat tempering oil and add the curry leaves. When leaves turn crisp and dark, pour the flavoured oil over the curry and cover. Mix well before serving. Serve with boiled rice.

Chicken Dhansak

PREPARATION TIME: 20 minutes

COOKING TIME: 40-50 minutes

50g (2oz) ghee or
45ml (3 tblsp) oil
1 onion, peeled and chopped
4 cloves garlic, chopped
2.5cm (1 inch) ginger paste
1.25ml (¼ tsp) turmeric powder
5ml (1 tsp) chilli powder
10ml (2 tsp) ground cumin
10ml (2 tsp) ground coriander
4 green cardamoms, ground
8 peppercorns, ground
2.5cm (1 inch) cinnamon stick, ground
2 tomatoes, quartered
1½kg (3lb) chicken cut into 10-12 pieces, ribcage discarded
65g (2½oz) toor daal (yellow lentil), washed in few changes of water
65g (2½oz) moong daal, washed in few changes of water
65g (2½oz) masoor daal (red lentil) washed in few changes of water
1 medium aubergine cut into 1cm (½ inch) cubes
100g (4oz) red pumpkin, peeled and cut into 2.5cm (1 inch) cubes
4 sprigs fresh methi leaves, chopped or
100g (¼lb) spinach leaves, chopped
2 sprigs fresh coriander leaves, chopped
45ml (3 tblsp) oil or melted ghee

900ml (1½ pints) water
Salt to taste
15ml (1 tblsp) brown sugar or grated jaggery
30ml (2 tblsp) tamarind pulp concentrate
1 onion, sliced and fried brown
1 lemon, sliced

Heat the ghee or oil in a deep pan and fry onion until light brown. Add garlic, ginger, turmeric, chilli, cumin, coriander, ground cardamom, peppercorn and cinnamon stick and stir fry for 1 minute. Add tomatoes and cook for 2-3 minutes. Add chicken and cook until liquid from chicken has evaporated (10-15 minutes). Add lentil, moong and toor daals,

This page: Chicken Makhani (left), Dum Ka Murgh (centre) and Chicken Dhansak (right).

Facing page: Goan Curry (top) and Pork Vindaloo (bottom).

has evaporated. Add tamarind pulp, yogurt, turmeric, black pepper, cumin, coriander, sugar, coconut and salt to taste. Mix well, cover and cook for 20-30 minutes. Add water if the mixture is too dry. Add green coriander and chilli. Cover and cook for 20-25 minutes or until pork is tender. The dish should have a smooth gravy. Serve with plain boiled rice.

Dum Ka Murgh (WHOLE CHICKEN OR CHICKEN JOINTS)

The recipe can be used for both jointed and whole chicken.

PREPARATION TIME: 30 minutes

COOKING TIME: 1 hour

1 onion, finely minced
10ml (2 tsp) ground coriander
5ml (1 tsp) chilli powder
1.25ml (¼ tsp) turmeric powder
15ml (1 tblsp) tomato purée
5ml (1 tsp) ginger paste
5ml (1 tsp) garlic paste
2.5ml (½ tsp) salt
150ml (¼ pint) natural yogurt
1½kg (3lb) chicken, cut into 8-10 pieces
Oil

Mix onion, coriander, chilli, turmeric, tomato, ginger, garlic and salt with yogurt. Rub the mixture onto the chicken pieces. Brush with oil and bake in an oven at Gas Mark 5 (190°C or 375°F) for 50 minutes – 1 hour, brushing with oil frequently, until the liquid has evaporated and chicken is cooked. For whole chicken, bake with above spices wrapped in baking foil for 1½ to 1¾ hours, then evaporate the liquid.

aubergine, pumpkin, methi leaves and fresh coriander. Mix well and add the water. Add salt. Cover and cook on low heat until chicken is tender (20-30 minutes). Remove from heat and take chicken pieces out. Mash daal with the aid of a masher or beat with an egg whisk until daal blends with water to form a smooth, greenish gravy. Add chicken and sprinkle with sugar or jaggery and tamarind pulp. Cover and cook for 10 minutes. Before serving, a little extra water may be used to thin down the gravy if it is thick. Before serving, garnish dhansak with onion rings and lemon slices. Serve with rice.

Goan Curry

PREPARATION TIME: 20 minutes

COOKING TIME: 1 hour

50g (2oz) ghee or
45ml (3 tblsp) oil
1 large onion, peeled and chopped
1 bayleaf
2.5cm (1 inch) cinnamon stick
5 green cardamoms
6 cloves
7.5ml (1½ tsp) garlic paste
5ml (1 tsp) ginger paste
8 curry leaves
450g (1lb) lean pork, cut into cubes
15ml (1 tblsp) tamarind pulp
150ml (¼ pint) natural yogurt
1.25ml (¼ tsp) turmeric powder
5ml (1 tsp) ground black pepper
5ml (1 tsp) ground cumin
5ml (1 tsp) ground coriander
2.5ml (½ tsp) sugar
15ml (1 tblsp) desiccated coconut
Salt to taste
150ml (¼ pint) water
2 sprigs fresh coriander, chopped
2 green chillis, chopped

Heat oil and fry onion until golden brown. Add bayleaf, cinnamon, cardamoms, cloves, garlic, ginger and curry leaves and fry for 1-2 minutes. Add pork and fry for 5-7 minutes or until liquid from pork

Chicken Makhani (BUTTER CHICKEN)

PREPARATION TIME: 20 minutes

COOKING TIME: 1 hour

150ml (¼ pint) natural yogurt
5ml (1 tsp) ginger paste
5ml (1 tsp) salt
1.25ml (¼ tsp) red or orange food colouring
1-1½ kg (3lb) chicken, cut into 8-10 pieces with skin removed
Oil
50g (2oz) butter
2.5cm (1 inch) cinnamon stick

6 cloves
6 green cardamoms
1 bayleaf
150ml (¼ pint) soured cream
1.25ml (¼ tsp) saffron, crushed
150ml (¼ pint) single cream
Salt to taste
10ml (2 tsp) ground almonds
1.25ml (¼ tsp) cornflour
15ml (1 tblsp) water

Mix yogurt, ginger paste, salt and red colouring and rub into chicken. Let it marinate overnight. Place in an ovenproof dish and brush with oil. Bake in oven Gas Mark 5 (190°C or 375°F) for 40-50 minutes. Save the liquid, if any. In a saucepan melt butter and fry cinnamon, cloves, cardamoms and bayleaf for 1 minute. Add soured cream and chicken liquid. Add crushed saffron, and single cream. Cover and simmer gently for 5-6 minutes. Add chicken pieces and adjust seasoning. Add ground almonds. Dissolve cornflour in water and add to the chicken. Let it thicken. Cover and simmer for 3-4 minutes. Remove from heat. Serve with nan.

Malabari Chicken

PREPARATION TIME: 20 minutes
COOKING TIME: 40-50 minutes

1 large onion, peeled and chopped
50g (2oz) ghee or
45ml (3 tblsp) oil
2.5cm (1 inch) cinnamon stick
6 green cardamoms
6 cloves
1 bayleaf
5ml (1 tsp) ginger paste
5ml (1 tsp) garlic paste
1½kg (3lb) chicken cut into 10-12 pieces
5ml (1 tsp) chilli powder
5ml (1 tsp) ground cumin
5ml (1 tsp) ground coriander
150ml (¼ pint) natural yogurt
5ml (1 tsp) salt
15g (½oz) coconut milk or cream
15g (½oz) blanched and sliced almonds
15g (½oz) raisins
120ml (4 fl oz) water
30ml (2 tblsp) evaporated milk
2 sprigs fresh coriander leaves, chopped (optional)
2 green chillis, chopped (optional)
225-240g (7-8oz) pineapple chunks

Fry onion in ghee or oil until tender (3-4 minutes). Add cinnamon, cardamoms, cloves, bayleaf and fry for one minute.

Then add ginger and garlic paste. Stir fry for half a minute. Add chicken. Stir and cook for 2-3 minutes. Sprinkle with chilli, cumin and coriander. Stir and mix well. Add yogurt and salt. Cover and cook for 10 minutes or until yogurt is dry and oil separates. Add coconut cream, almonds, raisins and water. Cover and cook for 20-30 minutes. Add evaporated milk and cook for 5 minutes. Add coriander leaves and green chillis and pineapple chunks. Mix gently and cook for another 5 minutes. Malabari chicken is a moist curry with thick, rich sauce. It is served with pulao rice.

Chicken Tikka

PREPARATION TIME: 10 minutes
COOKING TIME: 30 minutes

150ml (¼ pint) natural yogurt
5ml (1 tsp) chilli powder
10ml (2 tsp) ginger and garlic paste
10ml (2 tsp) garam masala powder
2.5ml (½ tsp) salt
1.25ml (¼ tsp) red food colouring
1½kg (3lb) chicken, cut into 6cm (2½ inch) pieces
Juice of 1 lemon
Oil
1 lemon cut into wedges

Mix yogurt with chilli powder, ginger and garlic, garam masala, salt and red food colouring. Pour over chicken pieces and mix well. Sprinkle with lemon juice. Mix well. Line the grill with baking foil. Arrange chicken pieces. Brush with oil and cook them under the grill for 4-5 minutes on each side. Brush with oil occasionally. Serve with wedges of lemon and a crisp lettuce salad.

Maach Bhaja
(MACKEREL FRY)

PREPARATION TIME: 10 minutes
COOKING TIME: 15 minutes

2 large mackerel, gutted and cut into 2.5cm (1 inch) thick slices
5ml (1 tsp) chilli powder
5ml (1 tsp) turmeric powder
5ml (1 tsp) salt
Oil for frying
Lemon juice

Wash fish thoroughly. Drain and dry well. Sprinkle with chilli powder, turmeric and salt. Rub in well. Heat oil and fry fish, a few pieces at a time, 3-4 minutes on each side. Drain on kitchen paper. Serve with lemon juice sprinkled over fish.

Sprat Fry

PREPARATION TIME: 10 minutes
COOKING TIME: 15-20 minutes

225g (8oz) cleaned sprats, washed and dried
1.25ml (¼ tsp) turmeric
5ml (1 tsp) chilli powder
5ml (1 tsp) salt
Oil for deep frying
Lemon juice

Rub sprats well with turmeric, chilli powder and salt. Gently heat oil and fry fish for 6-8 minutes, a few at a time, until crisp. Drain on kitchen paper. Sprinkle with lemon juice and serve.

Masala Fish
(WHOLE FRIED FISH)

PREPARATION TIME: 10 minutes
COOKING TIME: 15 minutes

5ml (1 tsp) ginger paste
5ml (1 tsp) garlic paste
5ml (1 tsp) salt
3 sprigs fresh coriander leaves, crushed
2 green chillis, crushed
5ml (1 tsp) ground black pepper
1.25ml (¼ tsp) turmeric powder
10ml (2 tsp) water
4-6 herring or rainbow trout, gutted, washed and dried
Oil
Lemon slices

Make 3 slanting slits on fish. Mix together the ginger, garlic, salt, coriander, chilli, ground pepper and turmeric powder. Add the water. Rub spices over fish and inside the cuts. Bake under grill for 10-15 minutes, brushing with oil and turning the fish occasionally until cooked. Garnish with lemon slices.

This page: Malabari Chicken (top) and Chicken Tikka (bottom).

Facing page: Main dish – top to bottom – Masala Fish, Maach Bhaja, Sprat Fry and Cod Roe Fry.

Cod Curry

PREPARATION TIME: 15 minutes

COOKING TIME: 20 minutes

50g (2oz) ghee or
45ml (3 tblsp) oil
1 large onion, peeled and chopped
2.5cm (1 inch) cinnamon stick
1 bayleaf
5ml (1 tsp) ginger paste
5ml (1 tsp) garlic paste
5ml (1 tsp) chilli powder
5ml (1 tsp) ground cumin
5ml (1 tsp) ground coriander
1.25ml (¼ tsp) turmeric powder
150ml (¼ pint) natural yogurt or
225g (8oz) canned tomatoes, crushed
1-2 green chillis, chopped
2 sprigs fresh coriander leaves,
  chopped

5ml (1 tsp) salt
450g (1lb) cod cutlets or fillet, cut
  into 5cm (2 inch) pieces

Melt ghee or oil and fry onion until golden brown. Add cinnamon, bayleaf, ginger and garlic paste. Fry for 1 minute. Add chilli, cumin, coriander powder and turmeric powder. Fry for 1 minute. Add either yogurt or tomatoes, chopped green chilli and fresh coriander leaves. Add salt and cover. Simmer for 2-3 minutes. Add 150ml (¼ pint) water. Bring to boil. Add cod. Cover and cook gently for 15-18 minutes. If tomato is used do not add any water. Serve with rice.

Prawn Curry

PREPARATION TIME: 15 minutes

COOKING TIME: 20 minutes

1 large onion, peeled and chopped
50g (2oz) ghee or
45ml (3 tblsp) oil
2.5cm (1 inch) cinnamon stick
6 green cardamoms
6 cloves
1 bayleaf
5ml (1 tsp) ginger paste

5ml (1 tsp) garlic paste
5ml (1 tsp) chilli powder
5ml (1 tsp) ground cumin
5ml (1 tsp) ground coriander
2.5ml (½ tsp) salt
1 green pepper, chopped into 1cm (½
  inch) pieces
225-270g (8-10oz) canned tomatoes,
  crushed
450g (1lb) large prawns, peeled
2 green chillis, chopped
2 sprigs fresh coriander leaves,
  chopped

Prawn Curry (left), Cod Curry (centre), and Fish Kebab (right).

Fry onions in oil until just tender (3-4 minutes). Add cinnamon, cardamoms, cloves and bayleaf. Fry for 1 minute and then add ginger and garlic paste. Add chilli, cumin, coriander and salt. Fry for half a minute. Add chopped green pepper and tomatoes, then bring to boil. Add prawns, cover, and bring to boil. Cook for 10-15 minutes. Add chopped green coriander leaves and chopped chillis. Serve with plain boiled rice.

Cod Roe Fry

PREPARATION TIME: 5 minutes

COOKING TIME: 15 minutes

225g (½lb) soft cod roes
1.25ml (¼ tsp) turmeric powder
5ml (1 tsp) chilli powder
2.5ml (½ tsp) salt
15ml (1 tblsp) plain flour

For batter
100g (4oz) baisen flour, sifted
1.25ml (¼ tsp) salt
1 egg, beaten
Water
Oil for deep frying

Put cod roes in a mixing bowl. Sprinkle with spices, one at a time, and add salt. Rub well so as to coat the roes thoroughly, then roll them in flour and keep aside. In a separate bowl mix baisen flour, salt, egg and a little water to make a smooth coating batter. Heat oil gently. Fry roes, a few at a time, well coated in batter, until crisp and golden. Drain on kitchen paper and serve hot.

Fish Kebab

PREPARATION TIME: 20 minutes

COOKING TIME: 15 minutes

275g (10oz) whiting or coley fillet
1 onion, peeled and chopped
2.5cm (1 inch) ginger root, peeled and finely chopped
1 green chilli, finely chopped
2 sprigs fresh coriander leaves, finely chopped
1 egg, beaten
10ml (2 tsp) garam masala powder
Salt to taste
5ml (1 tsp) ground black pepper
Juice of 1 lemon
Oil

Boil fish in water for 8-10 minutes. Cool and drain. Remove skin and bones and mash fish flesh. Add chopped onion, ginger, chilli, coriander leaves, egg, garam masala, salt, black pepper and lemon juice. Beat or grind into smooth paste. Make 10-12 equal-sized portions and pat each portion into a flat burger shape. Heat oil and shallow fry on each side for 3-4 minutes. Serve with onion salad.

Vegetables, Pulses and Chutney

Narangi Piyaz Salad (ONION AND ORANGE SALAD)

PREPARATION TIME: 15 minutes

2 large seedless oranges or
4 satsumas
6 spring onions, finely chopped,
   including green leaves
Salt
10ml (2 tsp) lemon juice
1.25ml (¼ tsp) ground black pepper
2.5ml (½ tsp) sugar
10ml (2 tsp) salad oil

Peel oranges and separate into segments. Cut each segment in two. Add onions, salt, lemon juice, pepper, sugar and oil. Gently toss to mix. Serve as a side salad.

Channa (CHICKPEA)

PREPARATION TIME: soaking overnight
COOKING TIME: 20-30 minutes

225g (8oz) chickpea
1.3 litres (2¼ pints) water
5ml (1 tsp) bicarbonate of soda
50g (2oz) ghee or
45ml (3 tblsp) oil
1 onion, peeled and chopped
1 bayleaf
2.5cm (1 inch) cinnamon stick
4 black cardamoms
5ml (1 tsp) ginger paste
5ml (1 tsp) garlic paste
5ml (1 tsp) ground coriander
5ml (1 tsp) chilli powder
1.25ml (¼ tsp) turmeric
5 fresh tomatoes, chopped or
5 canned tomatoes, chopped
1-2 green chillis, cut in half
Salt to taste
2 sprigs fresh coriander, chopped

Soak chickpeas overnight in 750ml (1¼ pints) water with the bicarbonate of soda. Drain chickpeas and boil in 600ml (1 pint) of water for 10-12 minutes in a pressure cooker. Strain and save the liquid. Heat ghee or oil and add onion, bayleaf, cinnamon and cardamoms. Fry for 1-2 minutes. Add ginger and garlic pastes. Fry

for 1 minute. Sprinkle with coriander, chilli and turmeric powder. Mix well and fry for half a minute. Add tomatoes, green chillis and chickpeas. Mix well and add 175-250ml (6-8 fl oz) cooking liquid. Add extra water if insufficient liquid. Cover and gently simmer for 10-15 minutes. Add salt and green coriander. The chickpeas should disintegrate when pressed between thumb and index finger. If not fully tender add extra water and cook further. Channa is a thick, moist dish. Serve with kulcha or nan.

Kassi Mooli (GRATED MOOLI)

PREPARATION TIME: 10 minutes

225g (8oz) mooli
Salt to taste
Juice of 1 lemon
1 green chilli, finely chopped
1 sprig fresh coriander leaves,
   chopped

Wash and scrape mooli. Wash again and grate. Keep on sieve and let some of the liquid pass through. Press and squeeze gently and put in a dish. Sprinkle with salt and lemon juice and mix in green chilli and fresh coriander leaves. Serve with daal and roti. Caution: mooli has a strong smell therefore always store well wrapped in cling film, in refrigerator.

Red Cabbage and Carrot Salad

PREPARATION TIME: 10 minutes

½ small red cabbage, finely chopped
2-3 carrots, peeled and grated
50g (2oz) raisins
5ml (1 tsp) sugar
1.25ml (¼ tsp) salt or to taste
150ml (¼ pint) soured cream
10ml (2 tsp) lemon juice

Mix cabbage, carrots and raisins. Sprinkle with sugar and salt and

pour over the well-stirred soured cream. Sprinkle with lemon juice and mix well. Serve with any meal as a side salad. In place of soured cream, plain salad cream may be used.

Lobia Curry (BLACK EYED LOBIA BEAN CURRY)

PREPARATION TIME: soak overnight and 10 minutes
COOKING TIME: 30-40 minutes

225g (8oz) lobia beans, washed and
   soaked overnight in water
600ml (1 pint) water
1 onion, peeled and chopped
50g (2oz) ghee or
45ml (3 tblsp) oil
1 bayleaf
2.5 (1 inch) cinnamon stick
5ml (1 tsp) ginger paste
5ml (1 tsp) garlic paste
1.25ml (¼ tsp) turmeric powder
5ml (1 tsp) ground coriander
5ml (1 tsp) chilli powder
4-5 canned tomatoes, crushed or
4 fresh tomatoes, chopped
Salt to taste
2 green chillis, halved and chopped
2 sprigs fresh coriander leaves,
   chopped

Boil presoaked lobia beans in 600ml (1 pint) water for 20 minutes. Cool. Fry onion in ghee or oil for 3-4 minutes. Add bayleaf, cinnamon, ginger and garlic paste and fry for 2 minutes. Add turmeric, ground coriander, chilli powder and stir the mixture well. Add boiled lobia and tomatoes. Add salt, chopped chilli and fresh coriander leaves. Cover and cook for 10-15 minutes on gentle heat. The gravy should be of thick consistency. Serve with rice or rotis.

This page: Narangi Piyaz Salad (top) and Red Cabbage and Carrot Salad (bottom) with Kassi Mooli.

Facing page: Lobia Curry (top), Razma (centre right) and Channa (bottom).

Aloo Methi
(POTATO AND FRESH FENUGREEK LEAVES)

PREPARATION TIME: 10 minutes
COOKING TIME: 10 minutes

50g (2oz) ghee or
45ml (3 tblsp) oil
5ml (1 tsp) cumin seed
1 pinch asafoetida (hing)
3 medium potatoes, peeled and cut
    into chunks

1 bunch fresh methi leaves, chopped
5ml (1 tsp) chilli powder
5ml (1 tsp) coriander powder
Salt
1.25ml (¼ tsp) turmeric powder
Juice of 1 lemon

Heat ghee or oil and add cumin seed and hing. When seeds begin to crackle, add potatoes. Fry and cook potatoes for 3-4 minutes then add methi leaves. Mix well and sprinkle with chilli powder, coriander, salt and turmeric powder. Stir the mixture to distribute spices evenly. Cover and cook on low heat for 6-8 minutes. Add lemon juice before serving.

Kachhoomar
(SHREDDED ONION SALAD)

PREPARATION TIME: 20-25 minutes

1 large Spanish onion, finely sliced
    into rings
1.25ml (¼ tsp) salt
1.25ml (¼ tsp) chilli powder
1 sprig fresh green coriander,
    chopped

Aloo Gajjar (left), Toorai Tarkari (centre) and Aloo Methi (right).

1 green chilli, chopped
15ml (1 tblsp) lemon juice
2 fresh tomatoes, chopped (optional)

In a dish put onion slices, salt, chilli powder, fresh coriander, green chilli and lemon juice. Mix well so as to release onion juice. Add tomatoes and mix well. Serve with meal or with kebabs.

Aloo Gajjar
(POTATO AND CARROTS)

PREPARATION TIME: 10 minutes

COOKING TIME: 10-15 minutes

50g (2oz) ghee or
30ml (2 tblsp) oil
5ml (1 tsp) cumin seeds
2 medium potatoes, peeled and cut
   into 1cm (½ inch) cubes
3 medium carrots, scraped and cubed
5ml (1 tsp) chilli powder

5ml (1 tsp) ground coriander
1.25ml (¼ tsp) turmeric powder
Salt to taste
Juice of half a lemon

Heat ghee or oil and add cumin seeds. When they begin to crackle, add potatoes. Fry for 3-4 minutes then add carrots. Stir the mixture and sprinkle with chilli, coriander, turmeric powder and salt. Stir fry the mixture for 1-2 minutes then cover and cook on low heat for 8-10 minutes. Sprinkle with a little water to help cook carrots. Sprinkle with lemon juice before serving.

Razma
(RED KIDNEY BEAN CURRY)

PREPARATION TIME: razma to be soaked overnight

COOKING TIME: 40-50 minutes

225g (8oz) red kidney beans, washed
600ml (1 pint) water
5ml (1 tsp) bicarbonate of soda
50g (2oz) ghee or
45ml (3 tblsp) oil
1 onion, peeled and chopped
2.5cm (1 inch) cinnamon stick
1 bayleaf

3 black cardamoms
5ml (1 tsp) ginger paste
5ml (1 tsp) garlic paste
5ml (1 tsp) chilli powder
5ml (1 tsp) ground coriander
5ml (1 tsp) garam masala powder
1.25ml (¼ tsp) turmeric
200g (7-8oz) canned tomatoes,
   crushed
Salt to taste
2 green chillis, halved
2 sprigs fresh coriander leaves,
   chopped

Soak kidney beans in 600ml (1 pint) water with bicarbonate of soda overnight. Next day pressure-cook in 450ml (¾ pint) fresh water (add extra water if some has been absorbed by the beans) for 5-8

minutes. Cool and strain, retaining the liquid. Heat ghee or oil and fry onion for 2-3 minutes. Add cinnamon, bayleaf, cardamoms, ginger and garlic pastes. Cook for 1 minute. Add chilli powder, ground coriander, garam masala and turmeric. Stir the spices well. Add tomatoes and salt. Add kidney beans and fry the mixture for 2-3 minutes. Add 175-250ml (6-8 fl oz) cooking liquid. Sprinkle with green chilli and fresh coriander leaves. Simmer for 15-20 minutes. Add liquid if gravy is too thick. Remove from heat and serve.

Saag Bhaji
(BRUSSELS SPROUT BHAJI)

PREPARATION TIME: 6 minutes

COOKING TIME: 10 minutes

50g (2oz) ghee or
45ml (3 tblsp) oil
5ml (1 tsp) five spice mixture (panch-
    phoran)
1 bayleaf
2.5cm (1 inch) cinnamon stick
450g (1lb) Brussels sprouts cut in
    half
5ml (1 tsp) chilli powder
7.5ml (1½ tsp) ground coriander
1.25ml (¼ tsp) turmeric powder
Salt
5ml (1 tsp) sugar
4 cloves, ground
Juice of 1 lemon

Heat ghee or oil and add five spice
mixture. Add bayleaf, cinnamon
stick and fry for half a minute. Add
Brussels sprouts. Mix well and
sprinkle with chilli powder,
coriander and turmeric. Add salt to
taste and stir well to blend all the
spices. Cover and cook on gentle
heat for 8-10 minutes, stirring the
mixture occasionally. Sprinkle with
sugar and ground cloves. Mix well.
Cover and cook for another 2-3
minutes. Sprinkle with lemon juice
before serving.

Toorai Tarkari
(COURGETTE CURRY)

PREPARATION TIME: 10 minutes

COOKING TIME: 15 minutes

22ml (1½ tblsp) oil
5ml (1 tsp) cumin seeds
225g (½lb) courgettes, peeled and
    sliced into quarter inch thick
    rounds
2.5ml (½ tsp) chilli powder
5ml (1 tsp) ground coriander
1.25ml (¼ tsp) turmeric powder
3-4 fresh or canned tomatoes,
    chopped
Salt to taste
1 green chilli, halved
1 sprig fresh coriander leaves,
    chopped

Heat oil and add cumin seeds.
When they crackle, add courgette
slices. Stir and sprinkle with chilli,
coriander and turmeric powder.
Mix well and add chopped
tomatoes. Sprinkle with salt, green
chilli and fresh coriander. Cover
and cook for 10-12 minutes.

Phalon-Ka-Chaat
(SWEET AND SOUR FRUIT SALAD)

PREPARATION TIME: 20-25 minutes

2 bananas, peeled and sliced
1 large guava, chopped
1 pear, peeled and chopped
225-275g (8-10oz) canned peaches,
    chopped, discard syrup
225-275g (8-10oz) canned
    pineapple chunks, discard syrup
1 small fresh pawpaw, peeled, seeded
    and cut into chunks
A few grapes, seeded
1 apple, peeled, cored and chopped
10ml (2 tsp) lemon juice
Salt
1.25ml (¼ tsp) ground black pepper
1.25ml (¼ tsp) chilli powder
Pinch of black rock salt (kala namak)

Put all the fruits into a large bowl.
Sprinkle with lemon juice, salt,
pepper and chilli. Mix well. Add
pinch of ground black rock salt
(kala namak). Mix and serve as a
starter, side salad or snack. Note:
many other fruits may be added
e.g. mango, kiwi, plum, lychees,
melons, etc.

**Pochari Kosambri (top left),
Kachhoomar (top right) and
Phalon-Ka-Chaat (bottom).**

Baigan Dahivaley
(AUBERGINE SLICES IN YOGURT)

PREPARATION TIME: 10 minutes

COOKING TIME: 10-15 minutes

5ml (1 tsp) chilli powder
1.25ml (¼ tsp) turmeric powder
1 large aubergine, cut into 5mm (¼
    inch) thick round slices
Oil for deep frying
225-275g (8-10oz) natural yogurt
5ml (1 tsp) garam masala powder
1.25ml (¼ tsp) salt
1 green chilli, chopped
1 sprig fresh green coriander leaves,
    chopped

Rub chilli and turmeric into
aubergine and deep fry aubergine
slices in oil, 1-2 minutes each side,
and drain on kitchen paper. Beat

yogurt and add garam masala
powder, salt, green chilli and fresh
coriander. Mix well. Arrange
aubergine on a flat serving plate or
dish. Pour yogurt over evenly.
Serve as a side dish.

Pachari Kosambri
(VEGETABLE, NUT AND COCONUT SALAD)

PREPARATION TIME: 20-25 minutes

100g (4oz) grated white cabbage
1 small onion, peeled and finely
    chopped
1 small apple, grated
1 raw mango, peeled and grated
Juice of 1 lemon
1.25ml (¼ tsp) salt
50g (2oz) fresh, grated coconut
1 green chilli, chopped
2 sprigs fresh coriander, chopped
50g (2oz) bean sprouts
½ cucumber, grated
50g (2oz) unsalted peanuts, skin
    removed

Put grated cabbage, onion, apple
and mango into a bowl. Mix well,
squeeze and discard excess juice.
Drain well. Sprinkle with lemon
juice, salt, coconut, green chilli and
fresh coriander. Add bean sprouts
and cucumber and mix gently. Add
lightly roasted and coarsely ground
peanuts. Mix and serve. Note:
other nuts, like cashews, chiroli,
pecan, walnut and hazelnuts may
be used. Grated carrots may also
be included if desired.

Green Bean Bhaji

PREPARATION TIME: 10 minutes

COOKING TIME: 10-12 minutes

45ml (3 tblsp) oil or melted ghee
5ml (1 tsp) urid daal
2-3 green chillis
6-8 fresh curry leaves
350g (12oz) frozen sliced green
    beans, unthawed
Salt to taste
15ml (1 tblsp) desiccated coconut

Heat oil or ghee and add urid daal,
green chilli and curry leaves. Stir fry
for half a minute. Add beans and
sprinkle with salt. Cover and cook
for 6-8 minutes. Sprinkle with
coconut and mix well. Cover and
cook for 3-4 minutes. Serve with
chapatis.

1 medium green pepper, seeded and
   cubed
225g (½lb) mixed frozen vegetables
Salt to taste
5ml (1 tsp) turmeric powder
5ml (1 tsp) ground coriander
5ml (1 tsp) chilli powder
3-4 fresh tomatoes, chopped
2 sprigs green fresh coriander leaves,
   chopped
1-2 green chillis, chopped

Heat ghee or oil and fry onion and
cumin seeds for 2-3 minutes. Add
potatoes and stir fry for 4-5
minutes. Add cauliflower,
aubergine and green pepper and
cook for 4 minutes. Add mixed
vegetables. Stir to mix well.
Sprinkle with salt, turmeric,
coriander and chilli powder. Add
chopped tomato. Stir and cover.
Cook on low heat for 5-6 minutes.
Add fresh coriander and chopped
chilli. Mix and serve. To make
moist curry add 150ml (¼ pint)
water after tomatoes are added.

Dum Aloo
(SPICED POTATO CURRY)

PREPARATION TIME: 10 minutes

COOKING TIME: 15 minutes

50g (2oz) ghee or
45ml (3 tblsp) oil
1 bayleaf
1 onion, minced finely
2.5ml (½ tsp) ginger paste
2.5ml (½ tsp) garlic paste
2.5ml (½ tsp) whole mustard seed
2.5ml (½ tsp) cumin seed
450g (1lb) small potatoes, with skins,
   washed and dried or
450g (1lb) potatoes, peeled and cut
   into chunks
1.25ml (¼ tsp) turmeric powder
10ml (2 tsp) ground coriander
7.5ml (1½ tsp) chilli powder
150ml (¼ pint) natural yogurt
1.25ml (¼ tsp) salt

Mushroom Aloo Bhaji
(POTATO AND MUSHROOM BHAJI)

PREPARATION TIME: 5-6 minutes

COOKING TIME: 10-12 minutes

50g (2oz) ghee or
45ml (3 tblsp) oil
1 onion, peeled and chopped
450g (1lb) medium potato, peeled
   and cubed
2.5ml (½ tsp) salt to taste
30ml (2 tblsp) garam masala powder
225g (½lb) button mushrooms, sliced
Lemon juice

Mattar Paneer (top left), Saag Bhaji (top right) and Baigan Dahivaley (bottom).

Heat ghee or oil and fry onion until
tender (2-3 minutes). Add
potatoes and fry for 5-6 minutes.
Sprinkle with salt and garam
masala. Mix well and cover. Cook
for 4-5 minutes until potatoes are
tender. Add mushrooms. Stir well.
Cover and cook for 2-3 minutes.
Sprinkle with lemon juice to taste.
Remove from heat and serve.

Mili-Juli Sabzi
(MIXED VEGETABLE BHAJI)

PREPARATION TIME: 15 minutes

COOKING TIME: 10-15 minutes

50g (2oz) ghee or
45ml (3 tblsp) oil
1 onion, peeled and chopped
5ml (1 tsp) cumin seeds
1 medium potato, peeled and
   chopped
3 cauliflower florets, cut into small
   pieces
1 small aubergine, cubed

Heat ghee or oil and add bayleaf
and onion. Fry for 3-4 minutes.
Add ginger and garlic and fry for 1
minute. Add mustard and cumin
seed. Add potatoes, mix well and
cook for 4-5 minutes, stirring
constantly to avoid burning.
Sprinkle with turmeric, coriander
and chilli powder. Add yogurt and
salt to taste. Mix gently, cover and
cook for 8-10 minutes until
potatoes are tender and most of
the liquid has evaporated. Sprinkle
with a little water if potatoes are
not quite tender. Dum aloo is a dry
dish with potatoes covered with
spices. Serve with puri.

Khata-Meetha Kaddu (SWEET AND SOUR PUMPKIN)

PREPARATION TIME: 10 minutes

COOKING TIME: 15-20 minutes

50g (2oz) ghee or
45ml (3 tblsp) oil
1 bayleaf
2.5cm (1 inch) cinnamon stick
6 green cardamoms
6 cloves
5ml (1 tsp) five spice mixture (panch-phoran)
2 medium potatoes, peeled and cut into chunks
450g (1lb) pumpkin, peeled and cut into chunks
5ml (1 tsp) chilli powder
7.5ml (1½ tsp) ground coriander
1.25ml (¼ tsp) turmeric powder
2.5ml (½ tsp) salt
10ml (2 tsp) sugar
15ml (1 tblsp) tamarind pulp
45ml (3 tblsp) water

Heat oil and add bayleaf, cinnamon, cardamom, cloves and five spice mixture and fry for half a minute. Add potatoes and fry for 4 minutes. Add pumpkin. Stir vegetables and cook for 3 minutes. Sprinkle with chilli powder, coriander, turmeric, salt and sugar. Stir the mixture to blend the spices. Add tamarind pulp and water. Cover and cook on gentle heat for 8-10 minutes until potatoes are tender. This is a moist curry without gravy. Serve with paratha or puri.

Palak Paneer (PANEER AND SPINACH)

PREPARATION TIME: 20 minutes and overnight for paneer. Follow paneer making recipe.

COOKING TIME: 10 minutes

450g (1lb) fresh spinach leaf (or well-drained, canned or frozen spinach)
50g (2oz) ghee or
45ml (3 tblsp) oil
225g (8oz) paneer, cut into cubes
1 onion, peeled and finely chopped
2.5cm (1 inch) ginger root, peeled and finely chopped
4 fresh tomatoes or
4-5 canned tomatoes, chopped
5ml (1 tsp) chilli powder
15ml (1 tblsp) lemon juice
5ml (1 tsp) ground coriander
25g (1oz) unsalted butter
1.25ml (¼ tsp) turmeric powder
1.25ml (¼ tsp) salt

Boil fresh spinach in 600ml (1 pint) water for 5 minutes. Drain and save water. Mash or purée spinach and keep aside. If canned or thawed frozen spinach is used, save liquid. Heat ghee or oil and fry paneer pieces until light brown. Remove. In the same oil fry onion and ginger for 3-4 minutes. Add tomatoes and sprinkle with chilli, coriander, turmeric and salt to taste. Cover and cook for 2-3 minutes. Add paneer, puréed spinach and lemon juice. If too dry use 45ml (2-3 tblsp) spinach water to moisten the curry. Remove from heat and serve with butter. This is a thick, moist curry.

Daal Pulses

PREPARATION TIME: 5 minutes

COOKING TIME: 10 minutes

225g (8oz) split or dehusked moong daal washed in 2-3 changes of water
600ml (1 pint) water
1.25ml (¼ tsp) turmeric powder
5ml (1 tsp) ground coriander
Salt to taste
1 small onion, peeled and chopped
50g (2oz) unsalted butter or clarified butter
1 green chilli, chopped
2 cloves garlic, peeled and chopped

To garnish
1 sprig fresh coriander leaves, chopped

Boil moong daal in water until tender and soft. Drain. Mash the daal with a potato masher or egg beater. Add turmeric and ground coriander and salt to taste. Simmer

This page: Khata-Meetha Kaddu (top), Palak Paneer (right), Dum Aloo (bottom).

Facing page: Green Bean Bhaji (top), Mili-Juli Sabzi (right) and Mushroom Aloo Bhaji (bottom).

until volume is reduced by ⅓rd. Fry onion in butter until golden brown, add chilli and garlic. Fry until garlic is browned. Pour over daal. Garnish with chopped fresh coriander. Serve with rice or chapatis.

Khari Urid Daal
(DRY URID DAAL)

PREPARATION TIME: 5 minutes

COOKING TIME: 10-15 minutes

225g (8oz) white dehusked urid daal washed in 3-4 changes of water
Salt to taste
200ml (⅓ pint) water

For garnish
1 onion, peeled and sliced
50g (2oz) unsalted butter
1 green chilli, chopped
2.5cm (1 inch) ginger root, peeled and sliced
1 sprig fresh coriander, chopped

Boil urid daal covered in water, with salt to taste, on low heat until water has evaporated. Fry onion in butter until golden brown. Add chopped chilli and ginger and fry for 2-3 minutes. Pour over dry daal. Garnish with chopped coriander. Serve with roti or paratha.

Masoor Daal
(RED LENTIL)

PREPARATION TIME: 6 minutes

COOKING TIME: 20-25 minutes

225g (8oz) red lentils
600ml (1 pint) water
5ml (1 tsp) chilli powder
10ml (2 tsp) ground coriander
1.25ml (¼ tsp) turmeric powder
1.25ml (¼ tsp) salt
1 sprig fresh coriander leaves, chopped
4 fresh tomatoes, chopped or 5 canned tomatoes, crushed
1 onion, peeled and chopped
50g (2oz) butter
1 green chilli, halved and chopped

Wash lentils in 4-5 changes of water, until water is clear. Drain. Add 600ml (1 pint) water and cover and simmer gently, without stirring, for 10-15 minutes until lentils are thoroughly cooked. Blend with a masher or beat with an egg beater. Add chilli powder, ground coriander, turmeric, salt,

Below: Sambhar (top), Masoor Daal (centre) and Arhar Toor Daal (bottom).

fresh coriander and tomatoes. Cover and simmer for 6-8 minutes. Remove from heat. Fry onion in butter and when brown pour over daal. Garnish with chopped chilli. Serve with rice or chapati.

Arhar Toor Daal
(YELLOW LENTIL)

PREPARATION TIME: 5-6 minutes

COOKING TIME: 20-25 minutes

225g (8oz) toor daal
600ml (1 pint) water
1.25ml (¼ tsp) turmeric powder
5ml (1 tsp) ground coriander
1.25ml (¼ tsp) salt
6 curry leaves
1 green chilli, split in half
15ml (1 tblsp) fresh or desiccated coconut
1 sprig green fresh coriander, chopped
5ml (1 tsp) mustard seed
50g (2oz) butter

Wash toor daal in 4-5 changes of water. Drain. Add 600ml (1 pint) water, turmeric, salt and coriander. Cover and simmer gently for 10-15 minutes until daal is well cooked and soft. Blend with the aid of a

masher or an egg whisk. Add curry leaves, coconut, chilli and coriander leaves. Cover and cook for further 8-10 minutes. Heat butter and fry mustard seed for half a minute. Pour over daal. Serve with rice or rotis. Toor daal should have a smooth, thick consistency.

Sabut Masoor
(WHOLE LENTIL)

PREPARATION TIME: 5 minutes

COOKING TIME: 20-25 minutes

50g (2oz) butter
1 onion, peeled and chopped
1 bayleaf
2.5cm (1 inch) cinnamon stick
5ml (1 tsp) ginger paste
5ml (1 tsp) garlic paste
225g (8oz) daal washed in 3-4 changes of water
450ml (¾ pint) water
5ml (1 tsp) ground coriander
2.5ml (½ tsp) chilli powder
1.25ml (¼ tsp) turmeric powder
3 fresh tomatoes, chopped or 3 canned tomatoes, chopped
1 green chilli, chopped
1 sprig fresh coriander, chopped
Salt to taste

Heat butter and fry onion until golden brown. Add bayleaf, cinnamon stick, ginger and garlic pastes and fry for 1 minute. Add drained daal and water. Cover and simmer gently for 12-15 minutes. The daal should be well cooked. Beat with a potato masher or egg beater to blend. Sprinkle with coriander, chilli and turmeric powder. Add tomatoes, green chilli and fresh coriander leaves. Season with salt. Mix well and cover and cook gently for 7-10 minutes. Remove from heat and serve with rice or chapatis. The daal should have gravy of medium consistency. If too dry, add a little water and boil for 2-3 minutes.

Sambhar
(DAAL AND VEGETABLE)

PREPARATION TIME: 10 minutes

COOKING TIME: 20-30 minutes

225g (8oz) toor daal
600ml (1 pint) water
1 carrot, peeled and sliced
1 potato, peeled and cubed
6-8 okra (bhindi), topped and tailed and cut into 2.5cm (1 inch) pieces
1 small courgette, sliced
1 small aubergine, halved and sliced
6 curry leaves
30ml (2 tblsp) tamarind pulp
1 green chilli, slit in half
Salt to taste
1 sprig fresh green coriander
15ml (1 tblsp) oil
2.5ml (½ tsp) mustard seed
1.25ml (¼ tsp) asafoetida (hing)

The following spices should be dry roasted and ground into a powder:
5ml (1 tsp) coriander seed
5ml (1 tsp) cumin seed
2 whole dry red chilli
10ml (2 tsp) channa daal
1.25ml (¼ tsp) fenugreek seed (methi)

Wash toor daal in 4-5 changes of water until water is clear. Drain. Add 300ml (½ pint) water, cover and simmer gently for 6-10 minutes. Remove any froth that forms. When daal is soft, beat with a potato masher or whisk. In a separate pan, boil all the vegetables: carrots, potatoes, aubergine, okra, courgette, with the ground, roasted spice and remaining water, for 4-5 minutes. Mix daal and vegetables along with liquid and stir gently to form an

Sabut Masoor (top), Khari Urid Daal (right) and Lal Mireh Aur Moong Phali (bottom).

Stuffed Peppers

| PREPARATION TIME: 20 minutes |
| COOKING TIME: 30-35 minutes |

50g (2oz) ghee or
45ml (3 tblsp) oil
1 onion, peeled and finely chopped
1 potato, peeled and diced
225g (8oz) mixed frozen vegetables
5ml (1 tsp) garam masala powder
2.5ml (½ tsp) chilli powder
10ml (2 tsp) dried mango powder
Salt to taste
6-8 small green peppers
Oil

Heat ghee or oil and fry onion until tender (3-4 minutes). Add potatoes and cook for 4-5 minutes. Add mixed vegetables, and sprinkle with garam masala, chilli powder, mango powder and salt to taste. Cover and cook gently until potatoes are tender. Remove from heat and cool. Wash and wipe dry green peppers. Remove top by slicing across to form a lid. Remove pith and seeds. Heat 45ml (3 tblsp) oil and fry peppers laid sideways, for 1-2 minutes, cooking on all sides. Drain well. Fill each pepper with filling and arrange them on a baking tray and bake in preheated oven, Gas Mark 3 (160°C or 325°F) for 20 minutes. Serve.

Aloo Gobi 14/7/07

| PREPARATION TIME: 10 minutes |
| COOKING TIME: 10-12 minutes |

1 large onion, peeled and chopped
75g (3oz) ghee or
45ml (3 tblsp) oil
2 medium potatoes, peeled and cut into chunks
1 medium cauliflower, cut into small florets
2-3 green chillis, chopped
2 sprigs fresh coriander leaves, chopped
3.75cm (1½ inch) ginger root, peeled and finely chopped
Salt to taste
Juice of 1 lemon
10ml (2 tsp) garam masala

Fry onion in ghee or oil until just tender, 2-3 minutes. Add potatoes and fry for 2-3 minutes. Add cauliflower and stir fry for 4-5 minutes. Add green chillis, coriander, ginger and salt. Mix well. Cover and cook for 5-6 minutes on low heat, or until potatoes are tender. Sprinkle with lemon juice and garam masala before serving. Serve with parathas.

even mixture. Add curry leaves, tamarind pulp, salt, chopped chilli and fresh coriander. Simmer for 10-15 minutes. Remove to a serving dish. For tempering, heat oil and fry mustard seed and asafoetida for half a minute and pour over sambhar. Serve with boiled rice.

Butter Beans and Green Capsicum

| PREPARATION TIME: 10 minutes |
| COOKING TIME: 10 minutes |

15ml (1 tblsp) oil
1 onion, peeled and chopped
225g (8oz) butter beans or broad beans
1 large green pepper, seeded and chopped
1.25ml (¼ tsp) turmeric
2.5ml (½ tsp) chilli powder
5ml (1 tsp) ground coriander
Salt to taste

4-5 fresh or canned tomatoes, chopped
1 green chilli, chopped
1 sprig fresh coriander leaves, chopped

Heat oil and fry onion for 3-4 minutes. Add beans and green pepper. Cook for 4-5 minutes. Sprinkle with turmeric, chilli and ground coriander. Add salt and tomatoes. Mix well. Cover and cook for 5-6 minutes on low heat. Add green chilli and fresh coriander. Cook covered for 2-3 minutes. If too dry add 30ml (2 tblsp) water. This is a dry dish.

Struthard + Melani
J Saturday

Nau-Rattan Chutney
(NINE JEWELLED CHUTNEY)

PREPARATION TIME: 20 minutes
COOKING TIME: 20-30 minutes

1 banana, peeled and sliced
1 apple, cored and chopped
1 large mango, peeled, stoned and
    sliced
3 rings of canned pineapple, chopped
200-225g (7-8oz) canned peaches,
    chopped
100g (4oz) dates, pitted and sliced
50g (2oz) ginger root, peeled and
    chopped
50g (2oz) raisins
175-200g (6-7oz) brown sugar or
    jaggery
2-3 dry red chillis
175ml (6 fl oz) malt vinegar
5ml (1 tsp) salt
2.5ml (½ tsp) cumin seed
2.5ml (½ tsp) coriander seed
2.5ml (½ tsp) onion seed
2.5ml (½ tsp) aniseed seed
50g (2oz) almonds, chopped

In a saucepan put all the fruits,
dates, ginger, raisins, sugar, chillis
and malt vinegar. Add salt and
simmer gently for 10-15 minutes.
Add coarsely ground, dry roasted
cumin, coriander, onion seed,
aniseed and almonds. Mix well and
cook for 5-6 minutes. Cool and
bottle. Chutney should be thick
and sticky.

Lal Mireh Aur Moong Phali Chutney
(RED-HOT CHUTNEY)

PREPARATION TIME: 5 minutes

1 large red pepper
3-4 whole dry red chillis
50g (2oz) unsalted peanuts
1cm (½ inch) ginger root, peeled and
    sliced
Juice of 3 lemons
Salt

Halve red pepper, remove pith and
seed. In a liquidiser, blend red
pepper, chillis, peanuts and ginger.
A few spoons of lemon juice may
be needed to blend the mixture.
Pour into a bowl. Add salt and the
lemon juice. Mix well and serve.
Red-hot chutney can be frozen.
Freeze in small tubs in small
quantities. Can be kept refrigerated
in sealed bottles for up to 2
months.

Dahi-Podina Chutney
(YOGURT AND MINT CHUTNEY)

PREPARATION TIME: 5-6 minutes

150ml (¼ pint) natural yogurt
20ml (4 tsp) sugar
10ml (2 tsp) dry mint powder or
2-3 sprigs mint leaves, chopped
Salt

Put yogurt, sugar and mint into a
liquidiser and blend for 1-2
minutes. Add salt and mix. Serve
with kebabs, samosa and pakoras.
Alternatively, blend in a bowl with
an egg beater. Ready made
concentrated mint sauce may be
used in place of dry or fresh mint
leaves.

Inset illustration, far left: Meethi Tomatar Chutney (top), Tmali Ki Chutney (right) and Dahi-Podina Chutney (bottom).

Main illustration: Chutneys. Adrak Khajoor Ki Khati Mithi (top), Nau-Rattan (right), Coriander, Green Chili and Coconut (bottom), Coconut and Urid Daal (left) and Red Pepper and Peanut (centre).

Tmali Ki Chutney (TAMARIND CHUTNEY)

PREPARATION TIME: 6 minutes
COOKING TIME: 10-12 minutes

225g (½lb) dry tamarind pods
100-175g (4-6oz) sugar or jaggery
1.25ml (¼ tsp) salt
5ml (1 tsp) chilli powder
5ml (1 tsp) cumin seed
5ml (1 tsp) coriander seed

Soak tamarind pods in 150ml (¼ pint) of boiling water for 5 minutes. Squeeze pods to remove soft pulp. Strain through sieve or squeeze by hand. Add little fresh warm water to the pulp and repeat, taking 3 extracts. The first one is the thickest and subsequent ones will be low in strength. Take 250-265ml (8-9 fl oz) thick tamarind extract. Discard the pods. Add to this extract sugar, salt, chilli powder and lightly ground, roasted cumin and coriander seed. Mix well. Adjust sugar and salt if necessary. Serve with kebabs. Tamarind chutney can be kept refrigerated for up to 1 month.

Adrak Khajoor Ki Khati Mithi Chutney (DATE AND GINGER CHUTNEY)

PREPARATION TIME: 20-30 minutes

100g (4oz) dates, sliced and stoned
50g (2oz) fresh ginger, peeled and cut into matchstick-size strips
100g (4oz) fresh, unripe mango, peeled and thinly sliced or
50g (2oz) dry mango pieces (aanchoor)
50g (2oz) raisins and currants mixed
25g (1oz) almonds, chopped
200ml (⅓ pint) water
175g (6oz) sugar or jaggery
1.25ml (¼ tsp) salt
5ml (1 tsp) red chilli powder

Put dates, ginger, fresh or dry mango, currants and almonds into a saucepan. Add water. Keep aside for 6-8 minutes. Add sugar or grated jaggery, salt and chilli powder and simmer gently. Cook for 15-20 minutes until chutney is thick and sticky. Remove, cool and serve. It can be bottled and kept with or without refrigeration for up to 3 months.

Meethi Tomatar Chutney (SWEET TOMATO CHUTNEY)

PREPARATION TIME: 5-6 minutes
COOKING TIME: 10-15 minutes

25g (1oz) ghee or
15ml (1 tblsp) oil
2.5cm (1 inch) cinnamon stick
1 bayleaf
6 cloves
2.5ml (1 tsp) mustard seed
5ml (1 tsp) chilli powder
1.25ml (¼ tsp) turmeric powder
50g (2oz) sugar
450g (1 lb) fresh or canned tomatoes
50g (2oz) raisins
2.5ml (½ tsp) salt

Heat ghee or oil and fry cinnamon, bayleaf and cloves for 1 minute. Add mustard seed. When they begin to crackle, add chilli, turmeric and sugar. Mix well and add tomato. Mix well and add raisins and salt. Cover and simmer for 8-10 minutes. Add a little water if liquid thickens. Tomato chutney should have medium consistency. Serve hot or cold. Once cooked it can be bottled or kept in refrigerator for 4-6 weeks.

Aloo-Mattar and Mirchi Bhaji
(POTATO, PEA AND GREEN PEPPER CURRY)

PREPARATION TIME: 15 minutes

COOKING TIME: 10 minutes

1 onion, peeled and chopped
50g (2oz) ghee or
30ml (2 tblsp) oil
2 medium potatoes, peeled and cut
 into chunks
5ml (1 tsp) ground coriander
5ml (1 tsp) chilli powder
1.25ml (¼ tsp) turmeric powder
225g (8oz) frozen green peas
1 green pepper, seeded and cut into
 chunks
225g (8oz) canned tomatoes, crushed
Salt to taste
2 green chillis, cut into quarters
2 sprigs fresh green coriander leaves,
 chopped
120ml (4 fl oz) water

Fry onion in ghee or oil until just
tender (2-3 minutes). Add
potatoes and fry for 5-6 minutes.
Sprinkle with ground coriander,
chilli powder and turmeric powder.
Mix well and add peas and green
pepper. Stir and add tomato and
season with salt. Add chopped
green chilli and fresh coriander.
Add water, cover and cook for 5-6
minutes until potatoes are tender.
The dish should have a thick gravy.

Bharey Bhindi
(WHOLE STUFFED OKRA)

PREPARATION TIME: 20-30
                                   minutes

COOKING TIME: 15-20 minutes

225g (½lb) bhindi (okra), washed,
 dried, topped and tailed
1 large onion, peeled and thickly
 sliced
75g (3oz) ghee or
60ml (4 tblsp) oil
10ml (2 tsp) ground coriander
10ml (2 tsp) ground cumin
5ml (1 tsp) turmeric powder
5ml (1 tsp) chilli powder
Salt to taste
15ml (1 tblsp) dry mango powder
15ml (1 tblsp) aniseed (sauf) powder

Split okra or bhindi halfway down.
Fry onion for half a minute in 1oz
ghee or 1 tablespoon of oil and
remove. Mix coriander, cumin,
turmeric and chilli powder, and put
a little of this spice mixture into the
split okras. Heat the remaining oil
in a frying pan or wok. Add stuffed
okras. Sprinkle with salt and stir
well. Cover and cook on low heat
for 5-6 minutes. Add fried onions,
then sprinkle with mango and
aniseed powder. Cover and cook
for 3-4 minutes. Serve with roti.

Tendli Bhaji with Cashew Nuts
*Tendli is an Asian vegetable that
looks like a gooseberry and tastes like
courgette.*

PREPARATION TIME: 10 minutes

COOKING TIME: 12-15 minutes

30ml (2 tblsp) oil
50g (2oz) cashew nuts
3-4 cloves of garlic, peeled and
 crushed
2.5ml (½ tsp) mustard seed
6-8 curry leaves
2-3 dry red chilli or fresh green chilli
225g (½lb) tendli, washed, dried and
 cut in half lengthways
Salt to taste
10ml (2 tsp) desiccated coconut
1.25ml (¼ tsp) turmeric powder

Heat oil and fry cashew nuts until
light brown. Remove, then fry
garlic until light brown. Add
mustard seed, curry leaves and red
or green chilli. Fry for half a minute.
Add tendli, sprinkle with salt and
stir the mixture. Sprinkle with
desiccated coconut, turmeric and
fried cashew nuts. Cover and cook
on low heat for 10-12 minutes or
until tendli is tender.

**This page: Aloo-Mattar and
Mirchi Bhaji (left), Bharey
Bhindi (centre) and Tendli Bhaji
with Cashew Nuts (right).**

**Facing page: Butter Beans and
Green Capsicum (top), Aloo
Gobi (left) and Stuffed Peppers
(bottom).**

Bread and Rice

Ubley Chawal
(BOILED RICE) 1

This method of cooking rice in a large quantity of water is very safe and ideal for all grades of rice, especially for starchy short and medium grades. Also for cooking large quantities as the fluffiness can be controlled. Use a few drops of lemon juice to whiten the rice.

COOKING TIME: 10-15 minutes

450g (1lb) Basmati rice
Pinch of salt
Few drops lemon juice

Wash rice in 4-5 changes of water until water is clear. Drain rice and put into a large pan. Fill pan with cold or tepid water 5-10cm (2-4 inches) above the rice level. Add pinch of salt and bring to boil gradually. When boiling, add drops of lemon juice, which bleaches the rice as well as cuts the starch formation. Boil for 7-10 minutes covered, or until the rice is almost cooked and has a hard core in the centre. Test by pressing a few grains of rice between thumb and fore-finger. Drain well and cover the top of the pan with a clean cloth or foil and put the lid on lightly. Replace on a very low heat. The moisture around the rice is enough to form steam and cook the core in 2-4 minutes. Serve with or without butter/ghee, with daal or curry.

Ubley Chawal
(BOILED RICE) 2

PREPARATION TIME: 5 minutes
COOKING TIME: 15 minutes

This method is good for long grain rice only, like Basmati, American, Deradun or Pahari rice. In cooking, the rice absorbs twice its dry measure of liquid. Bearing this in mind always measure rice with a cup or some such container and note. Then measure twice this amount of water.

450g (1lb) Basmati rice
Pinch of salt
Lemon juice

Wash rice in 4-5 changes of water until water is clear. Drain rice and put into a large pan. Fill the pan with measured quantity of water and let the rice soak for 10-15 minutes. The longer it stands the better the result. Add salt and lemon juice and gently bring to boil. Stir once or twice when boiling and cook covered until rice is almost cooked with a hard centre; about 7-10 minutes. Water should be totally absorbed. Do not stir rice during cooking. Keep on a low heat for a further 1-2 minutes to evaporate any remaining moisture and complete the cooking of the rice. Serve.

Sada Pulao (left), Meat Pulao (below, far left) and Ubley Chawal (below left).

Sada Pulao
(CUMIN FRIED RICE)

PREPARATION TIME: 5 minutes plus 15 minutes to soak the rice.

COOKING TIME: 15 minutes

450g (1lb) Basmati or American long grain rice
Water
75g (3oz) ghee or butter
5ml (1 tsp) cumin seed
1.25ml (¼ tsp) turmeric powder
5ml (1 tsp) salt

Measure rice with a cup and note. Wash rice in 4-5 changes of water. Drain well and add twice as much water as rice. Cover and set aside for 10-15 minutes. Heat ghee or butter and add cumin seed. Fry for a few seconds, do not allow to burn. Add strained rice, retaining water. Add turmeric and salt. Mix well and add strained water. Bring to the boil, cover and lower the temperature. Do not stir rice. Cook for 10-12 minutes until water is absorbed by the rice. Serve with any curry.

Meat Pulao

PREPARATION TIME: 15 minutes

COOKING TIME: 1 hour

1 small onion, peeled and sliced
75g (3oz) ghee or butter
2.5cm (1 inch) stick cinnamon
6 green cardamoms
3 large cardamoms
6 cloves
1 bayleaf
5ml (1 tsp) whole black cumin seeds
5ml (1 tsp) ginger paste
5ml (1 tsp) garlic paste
225g (8oz) lean meat, cut into cubes
5ml (1 tsp) ground coriander
5ml (1 tsp) ground cumin
150ml (¼ pint) natural yogurt
5ml (1 tsp) salt
450g (1lb) Basmati rice

Fry onion until golden brown in ghee. Add cinnamon, cardamoms, cloves, bayleaf and cumin seed. Fry for 1 minute. Add ginger and garlic pastes and fry for ½ minute. Add meat and sprinkle with ground coriander and cumin. Stir and add yogurt and salt. Mix well, cover and cook for 10-12 minutes until yogurt is dry and oil separates. Add 300ml (½ pint) of water and cook until meat is tender, 20-25 minutes. Remove from heat. Strain meat from its liquid. Take a large saucepan and add washed rice. Add gravy from the meat by measuring with the same cup. Use twice as much gravy as rice. If short, make up with water. Add the meat and the spices. Check for salt and adjust. Bring to the boil and then lower the heat, give a stir and cover and cook on low heat without stirring for 10-15 minutes until water is totally absorbed by the rice. Serve with a curry.

Biryani

There are two methods of making biryani; one with uncooked meat and the other with cooked meat. Both styles give equally good results but have slightly different flavours.

Method 1

In this method meat is marinated and cooked with semi-cooked rice.

PREPARATION TIME: 15-20 minutes and at least 1 hour for meat to marinate.

COOKING TIME: 60-70 minutes

275g (10oz) meat cut into cubes (leg or shoulder of lamb)
150ml (¼ pint) natural yogurt
5ml (1 tsp) salt
5ml (1 tsp) ground coriander
5ml (1 tsp) ground cumin
5ml (1 tsp) chilli powder
2.5ml (½ tsp) turmeric powder
5ml (1 tsp) ginger paste
5ml (1 tsp) garlic paste
2 onions, peeled and sliced
Oil for frying
3-4 green chillis, chopped
2 sprigs fresh coriander leaves, chopped
450g (1lb) Basmati rice
2.5cm (1 inch) cinnamon stick
6 small cardamoms
6 cloves
2 bayleaves
5ml (1 tsp) black cumin seed
10ml (2 tsp) salt
50g (2oz) ghee, melted
5-10ml (1-2 tsp) saffron dissolved in 90ml (6 tblsp) milk

In a small bowl, mix meat, yogurt, salt, coriander, cumin, chilli and turmeric powder, ginger and garlic pastes. Cover and set aside to marinate for at least 1 hour. For best results marinate overnight.

For boiling rice
Fry onions until brown and crisp in plenty of oil. Drain on kitchen paper. Put the meat and marianade into a large saucepan with lid. Add half of the fried onions, half of the chopped chillis and coriander. Mix well. In a separate saucepan, wash rice in 3-4 changes of water, add lots of water together with the cinnamon, cardamom, cloves, bayleaves, black cumin and salt. Bring to the boil. Cook for 3-4 minutes until rice is half cooked. Drain well and put the steaming rice over the meat. Sprinkle with the remaining fried onions, chillis

and coriander leaves. Make 5-6 holes with the handle of a wooden spoon for steam to escape and pour saffron milk all over the rice. Sprinkle with lemon juice and melted ghee. Cover with the lid and place the pan on the stove to cook over a moderate heat. As soon as steam is visible, lower the temperature. Cook for 45-50 minutes rotating the pan, so that all areas receive even heat. The rice will cook with the steam formed by the milk and yogurt and moisture from the meat. Lower heat to minimum and cook for another 10 minutes. Serve biryani from one end of the saucepan, mixing meat with rice with the aid of a spoon. Serve with a mixed vegetable raita.

Method 2

This method is the layering method. It involves two stages:

Stage 1
Cooking the meat

Stage 2
Layering the meat with rice

1 onion, peeled and chopped
100g (4oz) ghee or
75-90ml (5-6 tblsp) oil
5ml (1 tsp) ginger paste
5ml (1 tsp) garlic paste
275g (10oz) meat (leg or shoulder of lamb), cubed
5ml (1 tsp) ground coriander
5ml (1 tsp) chilli powder
1.25ml (¼ tsp) turmeric powder
5ml (1 tsp) ground cumin
150ml (¼ pint) natural yogurt
5ml (1 tsp) salt
2.5ml (½ tsp) saffron
15ml (1 tblsp) milk
1 onion, peeled and thinly sliced
Oil for deep frying
450g (1lb) Basmati rice
2.5cm (1 inch) cinnamon stick
6 cloves
5ml (1 tsp) black cumin seed
1 bayleaf
6 small cardamoms
10ml (2 tsp) salt
2 sprigs fresh green coriander, chopped
2-3 green chillis, chopped
Juice of 1 lemon

Fry chopped onion in ghee or oil until light brown in a large pan. Add ginger and garlic pastes and fry for another ½ minute. Add meat and coriander, chilli, turmeric and cumin powder. Add yogurt and salt. Mix well and cook with lid on

for 10-15 minutes until dry. Add 350ml (12 fl oz) water. Cover and cook for 8-10 minutes on low heat until meat is tender and there is approx. 120ml (4 fl oz) gravy left.

For rice
Dissolve saffron in milk. Deep fry sliced onion in oil until crisp and brown and drain on kitchen paper. Wash rice in 4-5 changes of water. Add plenty of water and add cinnamon, cloves, black cumin, bayleaf and cardamom. Add salt and bring to boil. Cook until rice is nearly done. The rice should increase in size but have a hard centre. Drain well, leaving whole spices in the rice. Divide rice in two. Line the saucepan base with half the rice, and top with the cooked meat, saving the sauce. Sprinkle with half the fried onion, half the fresh coriander and chilli. Cover with the remaining rice. Sprinkle top with the remaining fried onion, chilli and coriander. Sprinkle with lemon juice and saffron milk. Pour the meat gravy all round. Make a few holes with the handle of the spoon for steam to rise. Cover and put on gentle heat for 4-5 minutes. Mix from one end before serving. Serve with mixed vegetable raita.

Tahiri

PREPARATION TIME: 10 minutes

COOKING TIME: 20 minutes

1 onion, peeled and sliced
75g (3oz) ghee or butter
2.5cm (1 inch) cinnamon stick
6 cloves
6 cardamoms
5ml (1 tsp) black cumin seed
5ml (1 tsp) whole black pepper
1-2 bayleaves
100-125g (4-5oz) shelled or frozen peas
450g (1lb) Basmati rice washed in 4-5 changes of water
460ml (16 fl oz) water
15-20ml (3-4 tsp) salt

Fry onion in ghee until light brown. Add cinnamon, cloves, cardamom, black cumin, pepper and bayleaf. Fry for ½ minute. Add peas and cook for 2 minutes. Add rice and 460ml (16 fl oz) water and salt. Bring to boil. Cover and lower heat to simmer. Cook for 10-12 minutes until rice is cooked and water is absorbed. Serve with vegetable or meat curry.

Vegetable Pulao

PREPARATION TIME: 15 minutes

COOKING TIME: 15 minutes

450g (1lb) Basmati or any long grain rice
75g (3oz) ghee or butter
1 onion, peeled and chopped
2.5cm (1 inch) cinnamon stick
1-2 bayleaves
6 small cardamoms
4 large cardamoms
6 cloves
3-4ml (3-4 tsp) salt
Water
225-275g (8-10oz) mixed vegetables, sliced
5ml (1 tsp) ground coriander
5ml (1 tsp) garam masala powder
1-4ml (1-4 tsp) turmeric powder
5ml (1 tsp) chilli powder
Salt to taste

Measure rice with a cup and note. Wash rice in 4-5 changes of water, drain well. Heat ghee and fry onion until light brown. Add cinnamon, bayleaf, cardamoms, and cloves. Fry for 1 minute. Add mixed vegetables and fry for 4-5 minutes. Add rice and sprinkle with coriander, garam masala, turmeric and chilli powder. Mix well. Add twice the measure of water. Add salt to taste. Bring to boil. Reduce heat, cover and gently cook for 12-15 minutes, without stirring, until water is completely absorbed. Serve by itself, with a raita or with a curry.

Recommended vegetables:- Can be used in any combination.

1-2 aubergines, cut in 1cm (½ inch) chunks
1-2 potatoes, diced
1-2oz shelled or frozen peas
1-2 carrots, peeled and diced
2oz sliced green beans
1-2oz com kernels
2-3 cauliflower florets, cut into smaller pieces
1-2oz broad beans, frozen or shelled

Facing page: Vegetable Pulao (top), Khichri (left) and Shahi Pulao (bottom).

No leafy vegetables or pithy vegetables like marrow, courgettes, gourd etc. are advisable as they will make the pulao soggy. To colour the rice at random, do not use turmeric powder, but use food colouring, adding a few drops of any colour, at random, after the rice is semi-cooked and water is more-or-less absorbed.

Khichri
(KEDGEREE)

PREPARATION TIME: 6 minutes

COOKING TIME: 10-15 minutes

225g (8oz) Basmati rice
225g (8oz) red lentils
3-4ml (¾ tsp) salt, or to taste
2.5ml (½ tsp) turmeric
5ml (1 tsp) ground coriander
75g (3oz) butter
1 large onion, peeled and chopped
1-2 green chillis, chopped

Mix rice and lentils, measure with a cup and note. Wash in 4-5 changes of water. Drain and add twice the measure of water with the same cup. Add salt, turmeric and coriander. Bring to boil. Mix well by stirring gently. Lower the temperature, cover and cook over a gentle heat for 10-12 minutes until water is absorbed. In a frying pan, melt butter and fry onions golden brown. Add chopped chillis and pour over cooked khichri. Serve with poppadums and chutney.

Shahi Pulao
(NUT AND RAISIN PULAO)

PREPARATION TIME: 5-6 minutes.

COOKING TIME: 10-15 minutes.

450g (1lb) Basmati or long grain rice
75g (3oz) ghee or butter
2.5cm (1 inch) cinnamon stick
6 small cardamoms
2 large cardamoms
2 bayleaves
6 cloves
5ml (1 tsp) salt
Water
50-75g (2-3oz) raisins
50-75g (2-3oz) mixed nuts
    (almonds, cashew, pistachio)

Measure rice with a cup. Wash rice in 4-5 changes of water, drain. Heat ghee and fry cinnamon, cardamoms, bayleaves and cloves for half minute. Add washed rice,

salt and twice the quantity of water. Bring to boil gently. Stir once or twice. Reduce heat, add raisins and nuts, cover and cook for 10-12 minutes or until water is totally absorbed. Serve with meat or vegetable curry.

Jhinga Pulao
(PRAWN PULAO)

PREPARATION TIME: 6 minutes

COOKING TIME: 10-15 minutes

225g (8oz) long grain or Basmati rice
1 onion, peeled and chopped
75g (3oz) ghee or butter
2.5cm (1 inch) cinnamon stick
1 bayleaf
6 small cardamoms
6 cloves
5-10ml (1-2 tsp) ginger paste
5-10ml (1-2 tsp) garlic paste
225g (8oz) peeled and cooked
    prawns
15ml (1 tblsp) chopped fresh
    coriander
5ml (1 tsp) garam masala powder
1-2 green chillis
3-4ml (¾ tsp) salt

Measure rice and note. Wash in 3-4 changes of water. Drain and soak in twice the measure of water. Keep aside. Fry onion in ghee or butter until golden brown. Add cinnamon, bayleaf, cardamom and cloves, fry for 1 minute. Add ginger and garlic paste. Cook for ½-1 minute. Add prawns and sprinkle with coriander and garam masala. Add green chillis and salt. Stir in soaked rice and water. Mix well and bring to boil. Reduce heat, cover and cook until water is absorbed, about 10-15 minutes. Do not stir during cooking. Serve with curry. To colour pulao, add a few drops of red or orange food colour, 2-3 minutes before removing from heat. A pinch of saffron may be added along with the spices.

Pita

PREPARATION TIME: 10 minutes and 1 hour for dough to rest.

COOKING TIME: 30 minutes

10ml (2 tsp) dried yeast
5ml (1 tsp) sugar
Water
450g (1lb) refined or wholemeal flour
Pinch of salt
25g (1oz) butter or margarine

Mix yeast and sugar and add 30ml (2 tblsp) tepid water. Cover and let it rise. When it becomes frothy it is ready for use. Sift flour and salt, add butter and yeast mixture. Knead with water to make a pliable dough, cover and rest for 1 hour. Knead again and divide into 16 even-sized balls. Preheat oven to Gas Mark 5 (190°C-375°F). Roll each one out on lightly floured surface to a 15cm (6 inch) oblong or a circle. Bake in the oven on a tray for 7-10 minutes.

Saag Paratha
Paratha made with a leafy vegetable.

PREPARATION TIME: 10 minutes

COOKING TIME: 20 minutes

450g (1lb) wholemeal flour (atta)
Pinch of salt
75-100g (3-4oz) drained cooked
    spinach or
50g (2oz) boiled methi leaves
25g (1oz) butter
Vegetable ghee or butter ghee
Water

Sift flour and salt, add boiled spinach or methi and butter. Knead with water to make a soft, pliable dough. Knead well and rest for 5 minutes. Heat a non-stick frying pan or a Tawa. Make 16-18 even-sized balls. Roll each ball out onto a lightly floured surface into a 15-18cm (6-7 inch) circle. Place in Tawa. Cook for 1-3 minutes on low heat. Turn over and cook the other side. Apply vegetable ghee on both sides and shallow fry to light brown. Serve hot or cold.

Kulcha
Kulcha is yeast bread, deep fried.

PREPARATION TIME: 5-6 minutes and 5-6 hours for yeast to rise.

COOKING TIME: 3 minutes

5ml (1 tsp) dried yeast
5ml (1 tsp) sugar
Water
450g (1lb) rice flour
Pinch of salt
50g (2oz) ghee or butter
30ml (2 tblsp) natural yogurt
Oil

Take yeast and sugar and add 15ml (1 tblsp) tepid water. Cover and let it stand. When it becomes frothy it

is ready for use. Sift flour and salt. Add ghee or butter and yogurt. Knead with water to form a medium-hard dough. Make a well in the centre, add yeast mixture and knead. Let it rest for 5-6 hours in a warm place to rise. Knead again and make a soft, pliable dough. Make 20-25 even-sized balls. Heat oil and roll each ball into a 5-6cm (2-2½ inch) circle. Fry until lightly golden brown, about 2-3 minutes. Serve hot or cold with curry.

Stuffed Paratha

PREPARATION TIME: 10 minutes

COOKING TIME: 30 minutes

450g (1lb) wholemeal flour or
    chupati atta
Pinch of salt
25g (1oz) ghee or butter
Water
Ghee or oil for frying

Filling
A few florets of cauliflower, chopped
Pinch of salt
5ml (1 tsp) cumin seed
1.25ml (¼ tsp) chilli powder
5ml (1 tsp) ground coriander
Mix the above ingredients together.

Sift flour and salt. Add ghee or butter and knead with water to make a soft, pliable dough. Make 16-18 even-sized balls. Take a ball of dough, make a slight depression in the centre. Fill the centre with 5ml (1 tsp) of cauliflower mixture. Pull the surrounding dough from around the filling to gather at the top. Roll gently into a complete ball. On a lightly floured floor, roll each paratha into a 15-18cm (6-7 inch) round. On a preheated Tawa or frying pan, place the paratha. Let it cook for 2 minutes, until little brown specs appear. Flip over to the other side and cook for 2 minutes. Take a little ghee or oil and shallow fry parathas on both sides. Cook each side on low heat – until golden brown. Serve hot or cold with a curry.

Facing page: Biryani (top), Jhinga Pulao (centre left) and Tahiri (bottom right).

Nan

The actual taste of nan comes by baking the bread in a clay oven. Nan baked in gas or electric ovens does not have the same charcoal flavour.

PREPARATION TIME: 10-15 minutes and 2-3 hours for dough to rest.

COOKING TIME: 30-40 minutes

10ml (2 tsp) dried yeast
5ml (1 tsp) sugar
7.5ml (1½ tsp) bicarbonate of soda
Water
15ml (1 tblsp) sesame or onion seeds
450g (1lb) refined plain flour
Pinch of salt
25-35g (1-1½oz) butter, melted
60g (2½oz) natural yogurt

Mix yeast and sugar and add 15ml (1 tblsp) tepid water. When mixture becomes frothy it is ready for use. Sift flour and salt, add bicarbonate of soda. Make a well and add melted butter, yogurt and yeast mixture. Knead with sufficient water to give a smooth dough. Cover and rest to rise for 2-3 hours. Knead again and make 16-17 balls. Roll each ball into either an elongated flat bread – 15x25cm (6 x 10 ins) or a 15-18cm (6-7 inch) circle on a lightly floured surface. Coat with butter and sprinkle with a few onion or sesame seeds. Bake in oven, preheated to Gas Mark 6 (200°C or 400°F), for 5-6 minutes. When ready the bread will have brown spots on it. Serve hot.

Sheermaal

PREPARATION TIME: 10 minutes and time for yeast to rise.

COOKING TIME: 30-40 minutes

450g (1lb) self-raising flour
Pinch of salt
40ml (8 tsp) sugar
75g (3oz) butter or margarine
15ml (1 tblsp) dried yeast
1 cup tepid water
Milk
Sesame seed

Sift flour and salt, add 35ml (7 tsp) sugar. Add butter or margarine. Mix yeast with 1 cup water and add 5ml (1 tsp) sugar, mix and leave to rise. When frothy, add to flour. Knead with water to make a soft dough. Let it rest. When risen to twice its volume, knead again for 4-5 minutes. Divide into 10 equal

Below: Saag Paratha (top left), Stuffed Paratha (top right) and Kulcha (bottom).

portions. Roll each one out into a round or oblong shape of 5mm (¼ inch) thick. Brush with milk and sprinkle with sesame seeds. Preheat oven to Gas Mark 5 (190°C - 375°F) and bake for 5 minutes. Turn over and bake for a further 5 minutes until light brown and cooked.

Paratha

Parathas are shallow-fried breads.

PREPARATION TIME: 10 minutes

COOKING TIME: 25 minutes

450g (1lb) wholemeal flour (atta)
Pinch of salt
Water
Ghee for frying
Butter

Sift flour and salt. Add water and knead into a soft dough. Knead well and keep aside to rest for 5 minutes. Make 16-18 even-sized balls. Roll each ball out into a 5cm (2 inch) circle. Apply 1.25ml (¼ tsp) butter. Fold in half and apply a little butter and fold in half again to make a triangular shape. On a floured surface roll each into a 15cm (6 inch) triangle. Heat a

frying pan or a Tawa. Place the paratha on it. Cook for 1-2 minutes. Flip over and cook for 2 minutes. Apply a little ghee on the surface and flip over and fry first side again. Repeat for second side. Both sides should be browned and pressed with a spatula to cook corners. Make the remaining parathas up as above and stack them. Serve hot or cold with curry.

Facing page: Sheermal (top), Nan (centre) and Pita (bottom).

Roti/Chapati/Phulka

PREPARATION TIME: 6 minutes
COOKING TIME: 20 minutes

450g (1lb) plain wholemeal flour
(Atta)
Pinch of salt
130-175ml (4-6 fl oz) water

Sift flour and salt into a mixing
bowl. Knead to a soft, pliable
dough with water and leave to rest
for 5 minutes. Make 16-20 even-
sized balls and roll one ball out on
lightly floured surface to a circle of
18cm (7ins). Heat a non-stick frying
pan or Indian bread griddle known
as 'Tawa'. Place the rolled circle on
it. When little bubbles appear, turn
over and cook for ½ minute. Place
under preheated grill. The roti will
swell, turn over to the other side.
Make the rest in the same way and
stack them. A little butter may be
applied to keep the rotis soft on
one side. Keep them well wrapped
in a clean tea cloth or baking foil.

Alternative method:
The roti can be cooked for 1-1½
minutes on each side in the frying
pan until little brown specs appear.
Make them puff up by pressing
with tea cloth to rotate the steam.

Puri
*These are deep-fried, little, round
breads.*

PREPARATION TIME: 6 minutes
COOKING TIME: 10 minutes

450g (1lb) wholemeal flour or
chupati atta
Pinch of salt
50g (2oz) ghee or
45ml (3 tblsp) oil
Water
Oil for deep frying

Sift flour and salt and add ghee or
oil. Knead with water to make a
soft, pliable dough. Knead well and
allow to stand for 5 minutes. Make
25-30 small balls. Roll each ball out
into a small circle 5-6cm (2-2½
inches) in diameter. Heat oil, drop
in a tiny bit of dough. When the
dough surfaces immediately, the oil
is ready. If not then wait for oil to
heat to right temperature. Slide
one puri into the oil. Press gently
with a straining spoon. Turn over
and the puri will swell. It may need
a little pressing. Cook for 1-2
minutes until it is light brown. The
side of the puri which goes in first,
always has a thin crust, the other
side will always have a thick side.
When this thick side is light brown
the puri is cooked. Fry all the puri
and serve hot or cold with a curry
or chutney, or both.

**Roti/Chapati/Phulka (left),
Paratha (top left) and Puri
(above).**

Sweets

Saboodana Kheer (SAGO PUDDING)

PREPARATION TIME: 10 minutes

COOKING TIME: 10 minutes

½ fresh coconut, grated and milk extracted (see below)
900ml (1½ pints) milk
75g (3oz) sugar, or to taste
25g (1oz) raisins
50g (2oz) sago
8 small cardamoms, seeds removed and crushed
25g (1oz) almonds, blanched and sliced

Grate coconut and liquidize with 1 cup water. Strain to remove milk and discard the coconut. Boil milk to reduce to 1 pint, add sugar and raisins. Add sago and simmer for 5-8 minutes. Remove from heat, add coconut milk. Pour into a dish and add crushed cardamom seeds. Mix well and sprinkle with sliced almonds. Cool and serve.

Rasmalai

PREPARATION TIME: 15-18 minutes and overnight for paneer.

COOKING TIME: 30 minutes

1¾ litres (3 pints) of milk
Lemon juice
10ml (2 tsp) plain flour
8 green cardamoms, seeds crushed
A few sugar cubes, cut in half

For milk sauce
600ml (1 pint) milk evaporated to 450ml (¾) pint

For syrup
350g (12oz) granulated sugar
150ml (¼ pint) water

For garnish
A few drops of kewra or rosewater
25g (1oz) pistachio nuts, chopped
25g (1oz) almonds, chopped

Bring the 1¾ litres (3 pints) milk to the boil and add lemon juice. Leave the milk to separate. Cool for 10 minutes. Strain through a fine sieve or a new J cloth. Hang overnight for liquid to drain from paneer.

Make syrup by boiling sugar and water for 2-3 minutes. Mash paneer with the palm of the hand for 5 minutes. Add flour and cardamom seeds a little at a time, and continue mashing. Leave to rest for 2-3 minutes. Divide into 15-20 equal-sized balls. Take a ball and put a piece of sugar cube in the centre. Close the ball and make it smooth. Press gently to flatten it into a 4cm (1½ inch) round. Make all rasmalai like this. Simmer syrup and dip rasmalai in it a few at a time. Boil for 30 minutes. Keep milk sauce in a serving dish. Remove rasmalai from syrup and immerse in milk sauce. When all the rasmalai are in milk, sprinkle with rose or kewra water and chopped nuts. Cool and refrigerate before serving.

Gulab Jamun

PREPARATION TIME: 20 minutes

COOKING TIME: 30-40 minutes

450g (1lb) sugar
750ml (1¼ pint) water
Kewra or rosewater
20ml (4 tsp) self-raising flour
10ml (2 tsp) coarse semolina
25g (1oz) unsalted butter
135ml (9 tblsp) powdered milk
8 small cardamoms, seeds removed and crushed
Pinch of saffron
Milk
Oil or vegetable ghee for frying

Gently boil the sugar and water for 4-5 minutes to form 1 string syrup. Add kewra or rosewater. Mix flour, semolina, butter, powdered milk, cardamom seeds and saffron and knead with milk to form dough. Make 25-30 even-sized balls. Make the balls smooth and round or oblong. Attention should be paid to the split edges as they may crack during cooking; make them smooth. Heat oil or ghee and deep-fry gulab jamuns on low heat until dark brown on all sides. Drain well and transfer them to the syrup immediately. When all the gulab jamuns are in the syrup, give the syrup a final boil. Cool before serving.

Jallebi

PREPARATION TIME: 20 minutes and 24 hours.

COOKING TIME: 30-40 minutes

Batter
100g (4oz) plain flour
50g (2oz) baisen or cornflour
50g (2oz) natural yogurt
Warm water
Yellow food colouring
Oil for deep frying

Syrup
275g (10oz) granulated sugar
120ml (4 fl oz) water
A few drops of lemon juice

Prepare a thick batter with flour, baisen or cornflour, yogurt, and warm water. Set aside for 24 hours to ferment. Make 1 string syrup by boiling sugar: add lemon juice whilst syrup is boiling. Remove from heat. Take a piping paper and spoon in some of the batter. Pipe even-sized rings of the mixture into the hot oil and deep fry for 3-4 minutes, until crisp. Remove from the fat, drain thoroughly, and steep the jallebi in warm syrup for 3-5 minutes. Remove jallebi and arrange in a dish. Cook the remaining batter in the same way.

Shalu Tukra

PREPARATION TIME: 5 minutes

COOKING TIME: 10-15 minutes

6 white medium slices of bread
Oil or ghee for deep frying
100-175g (4-6oz) sugar
200ml (⅓ pint) of water
Few drops of kewra or rosewater
60ml (4 tblsp) condensed milk
150g (5oz) clotted cream
25g (1oz) sliced pistachio nuts
25g (1oz) sliced almonds
6 small cardamoms, seed removed and crushed

Deep-fry bread slices in ghee until crisp and brown. Drain on kitchen paper. Boil sugar and water for 2-3 minutes to make syrup. Add rose or kewra water. Arrange fried bread on a flat serving dish, pour sugar syrup evenly over the slices. Soak for 10 minutes. Pour milk evenly in the centre of each slice. Spread clotted cream next and sprinkle with nuts and cardamom seeds. Serve hot or cold.

Rasgulla (MILK BALLS IN SYRUP)

PREPARATION TIME: Overnight

COOKING TIME: 30-40 minutes

1.2 litres (2 pints) milk
Juice of 1 lemon
Kewra or rosewater
450g (1lb) granulated sugar
450ml (1 pint) water
10ml (2 tsp) self-raising flour

One day before, boil milk and add lemon juice. The milk will separate into curds and whey. Strain through a fine sieve or a clean J cloth. Discard the whey and suspend the curd overnight to drain off every single drop of liquid. Next day, boil rosewater, sugar and water and let it simmer gently. With the palm of your hand mash curds, or paneer, for 5-6 minutes to break tiny paneer globules. Sprinkle on the flour, a little at a time, and mix well, mashing with your palm. Let it rest for 1-2 minutes. Make 20-22 even-sized balls. Put a few at a time into the boiling syrup and boil for 10-12 minutes. Remove and place in a dish. Replace water which is lost by evaporation and repeat the process for the remaining balls. When all the rasgullas are done pour the syrup over them. Cool and serve. If a large saucepan is used, all the rasgullas can be made at one time.

Facing page: Gulab Jamun (top), Shalu Tukra (centre) and Saboodana Kheer (bottom left).

Facing page: **Mohan Thaal (top), Coconut Barfi (left) and Rasmalai (bottom right).**

Mohan Thaal

PREPARATION TIME: 10 minutes

COOKING TIME: 20-30 minutes

175-200g (6-7oz) sugar
120ml (4 fl oz) water
100-115g (4-4½oz) baisen flour
50ml (2 fl oz) milk
150g (5oz) unsalted butter or ghee
6 small cardamoms, seeds removed
   and crushed
25g (1oz) pistachio nuts, chopped
25g (1oz) almonds, chopped

Make syrup by boiling sugar and water until thick, or 2 string consistency. Mix baisen flour, milk and 50g (2oz) butter. Heat remaining butter, add baisen mixture and cook for 5-6 minutes. Add sugar syrup, mix well. Remove from heat, add crushed cardamom seeds. Mix well and pour over a greased dish and allow to set for 5 minutes. Sprinkle evenly with chopped nuts. Cut into pieces.

Balushahi

PREPARATION TIME: 15 minutes

COOKING TIME: 30-40 minutes

225g (8oz) plain flour
Pinch of salt
1.25ml (¼ tsp) bicarbonate of soda
65g (2½oz) ghee or unsalted butter
25g (1oz) natural yogurt
Seeds of 8 green cardamoms, crushed
Oil for deep frying

Syrup
225g (8oz) granulated sugar
50ml (2 fl oz) water
25g (1oz) pistachio nuts, chopped

Sift flour with salt and bicarbonate of soda. Rub in butter or ghee. Add yogurt, crushed cardamoms and sufficient cold water to make a soft dough. Divide into 16 equal-sized balls. Flatten each ball between palms of the hands to 'cakes' 4-5cm (1½-2 inch), with the sides thinner than the centres. Put into oil and deep fry on low heat for 8 minutes without disturbing. Turn them over and cook for another 8 minutes. Drain on kitchen paper. Make sugar syrup by boiling sugar and water for 2-3 minutes. Dip balushahi in sugar syrup for 3-4 minutes. Arrange on a tray and sprinkle with chopped pistachio nuts.

Above: **Balushai (top left), Gajjar Ka Halwa (right) and Pooa Kheer (bottom left).**

Paneer Ki Kheer

PREPARATION TIME: 2-3 hours

COOKING TIME: 1 hour

To make paneer:
900ml (1½ pints) milk
Lemon juice

Bring milk to the boil, add lemon juice. When milk separates, strain through a fine sieve or a new J cloth. Discard the liquid and suspend the paneer for 3-4 hours to drain out all the moisture. Break into small lumps.

To make milk sauce:
900ml (1½ pints) milk or
450ml (¾ pint) evaporated milk
75g (3oz) sugar or to taste
25g (1oz) chopped mixed nuts
6 small cardamoms, seeds removed
   and crushed
Few drops of rose or kewra water

Boil milk to reduce to 450ml (¾ pint); dissolve sugar and cool. (If using evaporated milk you will not need to add sugar.) When cold, add nuts and crushed cardamom seeds. Add paneer and refrigerate for 30-40 minutes. Add rosewater or kewra water. Serve.

Coconut Barfi

PREPARATION TIME: 20 minutes

COOKING TIME: 40-50 minutes

450g (1lb) desiccated coconut
450ml (¾ pint) evaporated milk
150-175g (5-6oz) sugar
225g (8oz) unsalted butter
8 green cardamoms, seeds removed
   and crushed

Dry roast coconut until pale brown. Remove from heat. In a non-stick saucepan, put the evaporated milk, coconut, sugar and butter. Cook on a gentle heat, constantly stirring the mixture, until oil separates, 10-15 minutes. Add crushed cardamom seeds. Cook until it is dry. Grease a flat dish. Pour mixture and flatten with a spatula dipped in cold water. Cool for 10 minutes and cut into squares or diamond shapes. Can be kept for 1 month in the refrigerator.

Gajjar Ka Halwa
(CARROT HALWA)

PREPARATION TIME: 15 minutes

COOKING TIME: 1 hour

1kg (2lb) carrots, grated
400-500ml (14-16 fl oz) evaporated
   milk
100-175g (4-6oz) sugar
2.5cm (1 inch) cinnamon stick
1-2 bayleaves
100g (4oz) ghee or unsalted butter
8 green cardamoms, seeds crushed
50g (2oz) blanched almonds,
   chopped
25g (1oz) pistachio nuts, chopped

Cook the grated carrots with evaporated milk and sugar on a low heat. Add cinnamon, bayleaves and cook until milk has almost completely evaporated. Add ghee or butter and cardamom seeds. Cook over a gentle heat, constantly stirring to stop mixture sticking to the pan. The colour should change from orange to deep red or brown, this should take 45-50 minutes. When oil separates, spread on a flat dish. Sprinkle with chopped nuts and serve. Can be eaten hot or cold.

Pooa Kheer

PREPARATION TIME: 10 minutes

COOKING TIME: 15 minutes

25-50g (2-4oz) plain flour
2 eggs
30-45ml (2-3 tblsp) water
25g (1oz) raisins
6 small cardamoms, seeds removed
   and crushed
Ghee or oil
25g (1oz) almonds, blanched and
   sliced
25g (1oz) pistachio nuts, sliced
Few drops rosewater
900ml (1½ pints) milk, boiled and
   reduced to 450ml (¾ pint)
25-50g (1-2oz) sugar

Mix flour, eggs, and water well to make a smooth batter. Add raisins and keep aside for 2-3 minutes. Add crushed cardamom and mix. Heat non-stick frying pan and melt a little ghee in it. Make 5mm (2in) pancakes. Make all the pancakes. In a flat serving dish, arrange all the pooas and sprinkle with almonds and pistachio nuts. Heat reduced milk with rosewater and sugar. Pour the milk over pooas. Serve after 5 minutes.

Glossary

Most of the items listed are readily available at supermarkets, health-food shops and Asian grocers. When they are not, substitutes can be made.

Aniseed (*Sauf*). These are the tiny seeds of the anise, and different from Chinese staranise. The Chinese staranise is called anise only because of its similar smell. Aniseed is used in curry powders, in making liquorice, cordials and cough linctus.

Atta. This ordinary wholemeal flour is easily obtainable from supermarkets, health-food shops and Oriental grocers. Whether white or brown, it is both nutritious and nourishing. The texture and colour differ due to the variety of wheat used. Extra bran added to the flour makes Indian bread dry and coarse in appearance. Always knead the mixture and allow it to stand for 5 to 10 minutes for the gluten to work. Atta can also be used mixed with baisen flour, cornflour, millet flour or any other kind of flour.

Baisen. Baisen is the flour of Bengal gram or black chickpea, also known as channa. The special, black chickpea is dehusked and then ground to make flour. It is very high in protein and is gluten free. The split pulse is used for making daals and the flour is used for making batter for pakoras and also for making sweets.

Bayleaf (*Tej Patta*). These are the leaves of a tree belonging to the common laurel family. Bay trees are used as ornamental plants and grow to great heights, even in Great Britain. The dried leaves are sold in all good food stores. They are used in sweets and curries and for pickling. Bayleaves should not be eaten.

Cardamom (*Elaychi*). There are two varieties of Elaychi. The first is small with green pods, which are called cardamoms or chotyenaychi. The seeds inside are dark and sticky, with a beautiful smell. Cardamoms may be included in recipes for the aroma they give to the food, or chewed after the meal as a mouth freshener. The skin of the pod is always discarded. The

Sevian Ki Kheer

PREPARATION TIME: 5 minutes

COOKING TIME: 15 minutes

25g (1oz) unsalted butter
1 bayleaf
100g (4oz) fine vermicelli
600ml (1 pint) milk reduced to
    450 ml (¾) pint
50-75g (2-3oz) sugar
8 small cardamoms, seeds removed
    and ground
25g (1oz) raisins
25g (1oz) almonds, chopped

Melt butter in a pan and fry bayleaf for 1-2 minutes. Add broken vermicelli and fry for 1 minute. Add milk, sugar and ground cardamom

seeds. Gently simmer for 5-6 minutes. Add raisins. Gently stir pudding once or twice during cooking to stop it burning. Remove from heat, pour into a serving dish, sprinkle with chopped almonds. Serve hot or cold.

Suji Halwa
(SEMOLINA PUDDING)

PREPARATION TIME: 5-6 minutes

COOKING TIME: 10 minutes

100-125g (4-5oz) coarse semolina
75-100g (3-4oz) unsalted or
    clarified butter
25-50g (1-2oz) mixed almond and
    cashew nuts
25-50g (1-2oz) raisins or sultanas

75-100g (3-4oz) sugar
250-300ml (8-10 fl oz) water
8 small cardamoms, seeds removed
    and ground

It is important to use a large enough saucepan as semolina will increase to twice its volume. Dry roast semolina in a non-stick pan for 2-3 minutes, until it turns light brown. Remove to a dish. Melt butter or clarified butter and add nuts and raisins. Fry for 1 minute, then add semolina. Add sugar and water. Sprinkle with ground cardamom seeds. Cover and cook on a low heat for 3-4 minutes. Mix well and stir fry for 1-2 minutes until dry. Serve hot or cold.

larger variety is black in colour with a thick skin. The seeds inside are used in sweets and are very different in smell and flavour from the smaller, green variety. Black cardamom is an important ingredient in the making of many curry powders, while both small and large varieties are important constituents of whole or powdered forms of garam masala.

Chilli (*Mirch*). There are many different varieties of chilli, but they only really differ in strength. Chilli powder is made by ripening the chilli on the plant and then drying it out in the hot sun, both skin and seed being powdered. There are a few hybrids which have the flavour but not the same pungency. These varieties are sold in European markets. Green peppers, or capsicums, are the large, fleshy varieties of chilli and are used as a vegetable. Paprika is made out of red peppers, or capsicums. Dried and then browned, paprika has the red colour and smell, but not the pungency, of chilli.

Cinnamon (*Dalchini*). Cinnamon is obtained from the bark of an evergreen tree belonging to the laurel family and is chiefly cultivated in southern India, Sri Lanka and the East Indies. The outer bark is stripped then dried; it has a pleasant, sweet taste and aroma and is thought by some to possess aphrodisiac properties. It is extensively used in sweets, pilaus, meat and other curries. It can be bought in stick and ground form.

Cloves (*Lavang*). Cloves are aromatic and may be used whole or in ground form. It is one of the spices which goes to make whole garam masala. Cloves are used for both sweet and savoury dishes. Oil of cloves is used in dentistry, to ease pain.

Coconut Milk. This is not, contrary to popular opinion, the liquid inside the fruit, which is more properly termed coconut water. To extract the milk, break the shell and extract the white flesh. Cut the meat into small pieces and blend with a little water in an electric blender. Let the pulp stand for five minutes. Squeeze the pulp through a sieve and collect the white liquid. The process may be repeated to produce progressively weaker milks. The used flesh should be discarded. If you cannot obtain fresh coconut, steep desiccated coconut in warm water and then strain.

Coriander (*Dhanai*). This is used to flavour nearly all curries. It is sold in seed and ground form, but fresh coriander leaves are also sold in some supermarkets, Chinese and Asian shops. The leaves are used for garnishing. Although it belongs to the parsley family it is different from both English and Chinese parsley in flavour.

Cumin (*Zeera*). Cumin belongs to the same family as aniseed. It has tiny, light brown seeds resembling caraway seeds. It is used in vegetable, meat and fish curries and in pickles. It is one of the most widely used spices. Ground cumin can also be bought.

Curry. For all curry preparations a range of spices is needed. It is advisable that you buy these individual spices and keep them in airtight containers. The flavour is in the aromatic oils that they possess. If the spices are to be used frequently then buy ready-powdered spices, otherwise buy in whole form and grind them freshly for use. Whole spices can be stored without losing much of their strength for surprisingly long periods of time. The overall flavour is better if you grind the spices yourself.

Garlic (*Lassan*). Garlic is sold in most food shops in either fresh or powdered or granule form. The fresh cloves of garlic give the best results.

Ginger (*Adrak*). Ginger is eaten all over the world. It is sold in fresh root form, dried form (called sonth) and ready ground. For best results use the fresh root, peeled and crushed or as directed.

Hing (*Asafoetida*). This is a gum resin and has a strong smell. It has medicinal properties and is used to combat nausea. Hing is always used with foods which ferment or are likely to produce gases, as it helps in digestion. Always buy it in a sealed jar or can. The powdered form loses its flavour much faster than the solid variety.

Jaggery. Sold in Oriental shops, this is the semi-solid stage of sugar-cane juice. It has a light yellow to dark orange colour and the flavour of molasses. Jaggery can always be substituted by soft brown sugar or ordinary granulated sugar.

Methi (*Fenugreek*). Fenugreek seeds are tiny, yellow seeds which are bitter to taste. The leaves are eaten in curry form as a leafy vegetable. Methi seeds are used in panch-phoran spice mixture and in many other curry powders.

Onion Seed (*Kalongi*). These are tiny, black seeds and are generally available only from Oriental shops. Onion seeds are used for curries and pickling.

Rice. There are many varieties of rice, but they are roughly divided into three groups: long grained like Basmati, American and Patna; medium grained like Carolina, and glutinous like Spanish and Chinese. The rice should be washed in three to four changes of water until the water runs clear, then soaked for ten to twenty minutes for the best results. To cook by the absorption method: measure rice with a cup and cook in twice as many cupfuls of water. This method is only good for long grained rice. The other varieties of rice should be cooked in large quantities of water and then strained. The rice should be drained and rinsed under hot running water. It is only loose rices which require washing and soaking; the pre-packed varieties do not.

Sugar Syrup. For various sweets different kinds of sugar syrups are needed. The strength is measured in 'strings'. Boil sugar and water for a few minutes, until it becomes thick. Take a drop of syrup between thumb and forefinger, press and separate; if the syrup forms one string it is called a 'one string syrup'. As it grows thicker it will form more strings. Three or four string syrup will be thick and sticky.

Tamarind. These are light brown pods which have a sour taste. To make tamarind pulp, take a little tamarind and break loose the pods. They sometimes have small, black seeds in them. Pour enough boiling water over the pods to submerge them. Leave for 10 to 15 minutes, then squeeze them well. The pulp around the seeds will dissolve in water, giving a darkish, thick, creamy extract. Strain this through a coarse sieve. This gives the first, and best, extract. For second and subsequent extracts, repeat the process. These later extracts are not as strong as the first. The trick is to make the first extract thick with the minimum of water and the remainder with varying strengths for future use. The extract does not last for more than four or five days and should be used within two for best results.

Once the pulp has been extracted, the pods and seeds should be discarded. Tamarind pulp can be bought in concentrated form from shops, and should be diluted before use.

Composite spices:

Ginger and Garlic Paste. Since ginger is used extensively in most meat, fish and poultry dishes, it is advisable to prepare the paste in large quantities and store it in a refrigerator in an airtight container. On no account store it in a metal container. Buy 100g or 4oz each of ginger root and garlic. Peel and cut into smaller pieces. Place in a blender with 4 fl oz of water. When reduced to a paste it will keep for up to a month in a normal fridge and much longer in the freezer. Wash the blender with a little vinegar or lemon juice before normal washing to get rid of the garlic smell.

Panch-Phoran. This is a mixture of five spices in whole form, mixed in equal quantities and on no account ground. To make a suitable quantity, which will keep for about six months, use: 5ml or 1 tsp each of mustard seeds (red and yellow), cumin seed, onion seed, aniseed and fenugreek. Keep the mixture in an airtight jar and use as required.

Facing page: Sevian Ki Kheer (top) and Suji Halwa (bottom).

Index

Adrak Khajoor Ki Khati Mithi Chutney (Date and Ginger Chutney) 45
Aloo Bonda (Potato Balls in Batter) 12
Aloo Gajjar (Potato and Carrots) 37
Aloo Gobi 43
Aloo-Mattar and Mirchi Bhaji (Potato, Pea and Green Pepper Chutney) 46
Aloo Methi (Potato and Fresh Fenugreek Leaves) 36
Arhar Toor Daal (Yellow Lentil) 42
Badam Ka Sherbet (Almond Sherbet) 10
Baigan Dahivaley (Aubergine Slices in Yogurt) 38
Balushahi 60
Bharey Bhindi (Whole Stuffed Okra) 46
Bhoona Gosht 18
Biryani 50
Blackcurrant Sherbet 10
Boti Kebab 18
Butter Beans and Green Capsicum 43
Channa (Chickpea) 34
Chicken Dhansak 28
Chicken Makhani (Butter Chicken) 29
Chicken Masala 26
Chicken Tandoori 26
Chicken Tikka 30
Chicken Tomato 26
Coconut Barfi 60
Cod Curry 32
Cod Roe Fry 33
Crispy Rolls or Curry Patties 12
Daal Pulses 40
Dahi-Podina Chutney (Yogurt and Mint Chutney 44
Dahi Wada (Daal Dumplings in Yogurt) 10
Dam Ke Kebab (Baked Kebab) 18
Dokhala 12
Dum Aloo (Spiced Potato Curry) 39
Dum Ka Murgh (Whole Chicken or Chicken Joints) 29
Dum Ka Ran 23
Egg Curry 16
Fish Kebab 33
Gajjar Ka Halwa (Carrot Halwa) 60
Ganthia (Baisen Sticks) 16

Ghoogni (Green Peas Fry or Spiced) 14
Goan Curry 29
Green Bean Bhaji 38
Green Mango Sherbet 8
Gulab Jamun 58
Jallebi 58
Jhinga Pulao (Prawn Pulao) 52
Kachhoomar (Shredded Onion Salad) 36
Karai Gosht 24
Kassi Mooli (Grated Mooli) 34
Keema Methi 18
Khageea (Spiced Scrambled Egg) 14
Khari Sevian (Savoury Mince Vermicelli) 12
Khari Urid Daal (Dry Urid Daal) 42
Khata-Meetha Kaddu (Sweet and Sour Pumpkin) 40
Khichri 52
Kofta Curry 18
Korma 26
Kulcha 52
Lal Mireh Aur Moong Phali Chutney (Red-hot Chutney) 44
Lassi (Yogurt Sherbet) 8
Lemon Sherbet 8
Lobia Curry (Black Eyed Lobia Bean Curry) 34
Maach Bhaja (Mackerel Fry) 30
Malabari Chicken 30
Masala Chops 23
Masala Fish (Whole Fried Fish) 30
Masoor Daal (Red Lentil) 42
Meat Do Piaza 24
Meat Madras 26
Meat Palak 26
Meat Pulao 49
Meethi Tomatar Chutney (Sweet Tomato Chutney) 45
Mili-Juli Sabzi (Mixed Vegetable Bhaji) 39
Mint Barley 8
Mohan Thaal 60
Mushroom Aloo Bhaji (Potato and Mushroom Bhaji) 39
Nan 54
Narangi Piyaz Salad (Onion and Orange Salad) 34
Nau-Rattan Chutney (Nine Jewelled Chutney) 44
Nimki and Papadi 16
Omelette 14

Pachari Kosambri (Vegetable, Nut and Coconut Salad) 38
Pakoras or Bhajias (Deep Fried Chick Pea Flour Fritters) 10
Palak Paneer (Paneer and Spinach) 40
Paneer Ki Kheer 60
Paratha 54
Passion Fruit Sherbet 10
Phalon-Ka-Chaat (Sweet and Sour Fruit Salad) 38
Pita 52
Pooa Kheer 60
Pork Vindaloo 28
Prawn Curry 32
Puri 56
Rasgulla (Milk Balls in Syrup) 58
Rasmalai 58
Razma (Red Kidney Bean Curry) 37
Red Cabbage and Carrot Salad 34
Rogan Josh (Rich Lamb with Nuts) 22
Roti/Chapati/Phulka 56
Saag Bhaji (Brussels Sprout Bhaji) 38
Saag Paratha 52
Saboodana Kheer (Sago Pudding) 58
Sabut Masoor (Whole Lentil) 42
Sada Pulao (Cumin Fried Rice) 49
Sambhar (Daal and Vegetable) 42
Samosa (Deep Fried Stuffed Savoury Pastries) 14
Sevian Ki Kheer 62
Shahi Pulao (Nut and Raisin Pulao) 52
Shalu Tukra 58
Shami Kebab 22
Sheermaal 54
Sheikh Kebab 22
Spiced Grape Sherbet 10
Sprat Fry 30
Stuffed Paratha 52
Stuffed Peppers 43
Suji Halwa (Semolina Pudding) 62
Tahiri 50
Tandi Masala Chaaey (Spiced Iced Tea) 8
Tali Kaleji/Gurda/Dil (Mixed Fry) 23
Tendli Bhaji with Cashew Nuts 46
Tikia (Potato Mince Patties) 14
Tmali Ki Chutney (Tamarind Chutney) 45
Toorai Tarkari (Courgette Curry) 38
Ubley Chawal (Boiled Rice) 48
Vegetable Pulao 50
Wada (Daal Fritters) 14